Skinny House

Julie L. Seely

A Skinny House Press™ Book

An Imprint of Skinny House Productions LLC

44050 Ashburn Plaza, Ste. 195-649 Ashburn, Virginia 20147

www.skinnyhouse.org

Names: Seely, Julie L., 1956-, author.

Title: Skinny house : a memoir of family / Julie Seely.

Description: Ashburn, Virginia : Skinny House Productions, LLC, [2018] | Includes bibliographical references and index.

Identifiers: ISBN: 978-0-9968777-0-1 (paperback) | 978-0-9968777-1-8 (ePub) | 978-0-9968777-2-5 (Mobi) | LCCN: 2018908542

Subjects: LCSH: Seely, Julie L, 1956- Family--Biography. | Seely, Nathan Thomas, 1893-1962. | Small houses--New York (State)--Mamaroneck. | Historic buildings--New York (State)-- Mamaroneck. | African American families--New York (State)--1919-1933. | African American families--New York (State)--1933-1945. | African American families--New York (State)-- Mamaroneck--History. | Migration, Internal--United States. | Depressions--1929--New York (State).

Classification: LCC: NA7533 .S44 2018 | DDC: 728.3--dc23

Unless otherwise noted, all photos appear courtesy of Julie Seely.

Printed in the United States of America.

Skinny House

A Memoir of Family

Julie L. Seely

Skinny House Press™

Virginia

This book is dedicated to my mother Doris and sister Diane.

Contents

Ambidextrous

Changing Times

Rising Phoenix

What About the Children?

Legacy

Addenda

Foreword

DESPITE ITS TITLE, THIS BOOK is no simple story about an odd narrow-built dwelling. It's about the family who lived in the house and the patriarch who built it.

Located at 175 Grand Street in Mamaroneck, New York, the three-story house, nestled between full-sized homes, is just ten feet wide. Known locally as the "Skinny House," the curious structure was built by an ambitious black carpenter who owned a successful construction business in the Roaring Twenties.

Nathan Seely and the house he built are the foundation upon which his granddaughter, Julie Seely, tells the story of three generations of her family, both its high and lows.

Julie gives voice and personality to Skinny House, a property with a story to tell. Nathan built it with his own hands, using salvaged materials.

It's a story of a proud man who loses his business and dream house and builds Skinny House to shield his wife and two children from the calamity of the Great Depression. Julie reveals the travails that caused conflict between husband and wife and fissures between father and son. She shows the centrifugal force of the Depression on one struggling American family.

Julie's research began in 2010 with the discovery of a 1925 brochure of her grandfather's business. She knew next to nothing about the man. He died when she was a child. In a quest to learn more, she exhumed secrets buried by her father, Tom, who was estranged from his father. The two men never reconciled. A physician by training, Julie missed the chance to practice generational healing while her father still lived.

— Gary Rawlins, journalist and family friend

Introduction

THIS IS A STORY ABOUT a family whose lives were affected by historical events. Although I have the advantage of hindsight and access to research by experts, I am no historian. However, I feel compelled to include historical context in many chapters to gain insight into why my grandfather Nathan Seely, an African-American contractor in Mamaroneck, New York, and his son, Tom, my father, came to make certain decisions they felt were best for their families at the time.

Nathan's story spans two polarizing decades in American history—the prosperous times of the Roaring Twenties and the devastating years of the Great Depression. In the 1920s, times were good for my grandfather and his business. The national unemployment rate was low and family incomes were stable. Credit was easy to secure and bank loans were abundant, even for a few black folks. The construction industry was robust and its profits high.

A short decade later, toward 1929 and for most of the 1930s, America was on its knees. The financial ruin of thousands of businesses fueled massive unemployment. The mood of the country was one of desperation and isolation where every man had to fend for himself. African-Americans were worse off than whites. According to Cheryl Greenberg's book *To Ask for an Equal Chance*, blacks had already been living in poverty in most sections of the country prior to the Depression. They became the last folks hired and the first fired, even for the most menial jobs.[1]

My father, Tom, grew up during this very turbulent period. The central part of this book is about his adolescent life and times when he lived in a very skinny house my grandfather built on Grand Street in Mamaroneck. The story transitions to my father's life away from Mamaroneck during the 1940s when he pursued an education, a career, and marriage. In his mind, however, the memories of living in the Skinny House were constant companions.

The last few chapters covering the 1960s and 1970s are an attempt to understand how the legacies of my grandfather and father have influenced my life growing up in Baltimore, Maryland.

The primary resources used for this book were limited since many of the family members I write about died many years ago. My grandparents Nathan and Lillian, parents Tom and Doris, and my paternal Aunt Sug are all deceased. I was fortunate, however, to spend much of the past five years interviewing my mother about her experiences living in the Skinny House before she died in January 2016. She had much to say about my grandfather, his family, and about being married to my father. Throughout this journey I became an explorer seeking the truest story possible, considering a lot of the intimate details I obtained about my grandfather were obtained secondhand.

Objective sources for this book included Westchester County land records, *Gannett* and *New York Times* newspaper articles, United States Census reports, draft records, and genealogy research from Ancestry. com. In the 1920s and 1930s, the US Census records were handwritten, sometimes illegible, and fraught with misspellings of names and inaccurate ages. Some of the recorded land transfers were confusing and required much time and effort to sort out. I elicited the assistance of a New York state historian-researcher to affirm the sequence of land purchases by Nathan and his brother and business partner, my great-uncle Willard Seely. Why was this so important to me? It was clear that investing in real estate was very important to Nathan and Willard. The least I could do was aim to be as accurate as possible in retelling their story.

Through each decade, the legacies of my grandfather and father have traveled with me. As an adult, my life has been easy compared to the road they traveled. I always assumed that I would go to college, that I would have a nice home, and that I would have financial security. My grandfather and father made no such assumptions that they would have a good life. They struggled for everything they had. I have come to understand that I owe my good life to their hard work and perseverance. I am grateful also for the odd-looking house my grandfather built, now nicknamed the Skinny House, for it has provided a window into their past lives and has inspired a new generation of history seekers within our family.

Julie L. Seely
www.skinnyhouse.org

Focus on the
talents you have
and not on those
you don't have.
What appears to
be a handicap may
be your blessing in
disguise. Build around obstacles.
Salvage what you can. If you
cannot build out, build up. Music
can bring you great comfort and
joy. Only you can decide what your
dreams are made of. You can be a star
and write your own press releases.
**It is not the size of your house that
matters. What matters is the size of
the heart and soul you put into that
house to make it your home.** The
decisions you make now will affect
your children and grandchildren.

The Skinny House of Lessons
Illustration by Dashton Parham

"You may have a fresh start any moment you choose, for this thing we call 'failure' is not the falling down, but the staying down."

Mary Pickford
1892–1979
Hollywood actress

Ambidextrous

I

THE SKINNY HOUSE

Shadow and Light

JUST OUTSIDE NEW YORK CITY, in Westchester County in the Village of Mamaroneck at 175 Grand Street, there stands an odd, whimsical-looking house known as the "Skinny House." My grandfather, Nathan Seely, built the house in 1932 during the Great Depression. The house still stands.

For decades, his ten-foot-wide, three-story, single-family home has captured the curiosity of people from as far away as Europe. It has been the subject of newspaper articles, artist renderings, poems, a documentary, and countless elementary school book reports.

While the newspaper articles over the years have focused on the architectural details of this unconventional home, the poignant story of Nathan and his family—his wife Lillian, daughter Sug, and son Tom—has never been told.

There are a couple of reasons Nathan's story has remained untold for so long. For one, my grandfather passed away in 1962 at the age of sixty-nine, long before his house became famous. From what I have learned about him, I surmise that had he lived into the 1970s when the first newspaper articles appeared about the Skinny House, he would have gladly shared with the public all the colorful details about building his one-of-a-kind home. My grandmother Lillian, in contrast to my grandfather's openness, was fiercely protective of her privacy. She lived alone in the house until 1986 and I suspect all those years she felt exposed and vulnerable with the curiosity seekers and tourists who cruised by the property and often ventured up to her living room window to peek inside.

However, the main reason the backstory of the Skinny House has not been told is because of my father, Tom. He lived in the house from his childhood in the 1930s until he was a young adult during the 1940s. He had a secret.

My father rarely spoke to us about growing up in the Skinny House, and he spoke even less about Nathan. He left Mamaroneck in 1941 and essentially buried his memories. Growing up in Baltimore, my siblings and I were respectful of Dad's sensitivity about the matter and his silence. We found it strange, however, that he would stammer and stutter anytime he met someone who grew up near Mamaroneck. When I was older, I realized that he was afraid the native might discover that he had grown up in "that" house, and it would be only a matter of seconds before the ground would split open and swallow him up. Dad's anxious reaction and dark, heavy silence was an invisible, yet onerous, burden for all of us. I found myself absorbing some of his silence about the house and the grandfather whom I had never met. I never really understood the reasons why I felt this way. I figured my grandfather Nathan must have done something wrong, but I could not figure out what.

As a child and young adult, I never took much interest in the house either. Mamaroneck was miles away from our life in Baltimore. Out of sight and out of mind. The Skinny House was simply my grandmother's home—a place we visited on holidays, and a place where she spoiled us kids with coffee cake and coffee ice cream. The Skinny House was our cozy theater where we watched with amazement as she sipped steaming hot coffee from a saucer instead of a cup. She entertained us and we loved her.

It was not until decades later, long after my grandparents and father had passed away and I had my own child, that my curiosity about my grandfather and his life intensified. It happened in 1998 when I was a young, divorced physician trying to juggle my personal life with building an obstetrics and gynecology practice in a Baltimore suburb. My son, Devereaux, was in third grade when his teacher recruited parents to come to class and share generational family stories. Like many parents, I shuddered at the thought of standing before a group of eight-year-olds with the goal of entertaining them, much less teaching them anything. However, as a parent, I realized it was no longer just about me.

I remembered my Aunt Sug had given me several file boxes containing Skinny House artifacts and family memorabilia. She was the kind of person who saved everything. After the Skinny House was sold out of the family in 1986 and my father died in 1989, I had stored those boxes of Mamaroneck memories deep in the basement of my small Baltimore row house where we were living at the time. I was waiting until Dad's kryptonite had faded and I could pick them up and embrace them without feeling weak and vulnerable too. Now, despite misgivings, I went in search of them.

I found the boxes just where I had left them, stacked in a corner of the basement blessed with dust and a pile of old coats that I had promised to Goodwill but had never delivered. I opened the first box and sneezed a hundred times, wondering just how long I would survive after inhaling a cloud of mold and mildew.

I sifted through familiar, faded black-and-white photographs of the Skinny House and of my father's family. This time I looked at the photographs from a fresh perspective. I noticed a few things that piqued my curiosity. My grandfather, usually dressed in construction overalls, had a prideful and engaging smile. He looked as if he was explaining something to you and giving you his undivided attention. My grandmother Lillian wore lipstick and pearls in most of the photographs, her hand often propped on her hip just to emphasize her point. Her stance alone would make you think twice about challenging anything she had to say, regardless of whether or not she had a newly starched apron tied around her waist. Aunt Sug, pretty and poised, always had a confident and sunny smile. She looked as if she could break out into song and dance at a moment's notice. However, I noticed that in most of the early photographs of my father, he had a pensive and sad expression. I rarely found a photograph of him smiling.

All the photographs seemed like important clues about the personalities within my father's family, and I wanted to know more. I knew some basic facts about my grandfather. Like many Americans during the Great Depression, Nathan found himself desperate and destitute after losing his contracting business to bankruptcy and his home to foreclosure. He was forced to come up with a plan to keep a roof over his head. Had he not done so, my father would have grown up homeless.

According to the story passed down to me, my grandfather had done more than just come up with a plan. In 1932, he drafted a blueprint and single-handedly built a ten-foot-wide, three-story house of salvaged materials for his family. According to local newspaper accounts after 1986, he built the house on a narrow plot of land donated by his neighbor. I had always thought the account of this event was not noteworthy, but I have discovered since then that there was much more to the story.

In one of the boxes I found the blueprint of the Skinny House and I was quite pleased. I was sure the blueprint would be the highlight of the presentation for Devereaux's class. However, there was another item that caught my eye. It was a tattered orange brochure titled *Homes for Colored People* and was clearly a marketing publication for Seely Bros., Inc., my grandfather's contracting business.

How could I have grown up and not known of my grandfather's business or his aspirations to become a builder of homes for black people? The answer was simple. I had not asked many questions about Nathan, since the very mention of his name seemed to make my father wince. The boxes in the basement, I realized, were stuffed with my family's legacy.

Pulling from the documents I had discovered, I shared the pictures and story of my grandfather, my father, and the Skinny House with Devereaux and his classmates. To this day, I have no idea whether any of those kids, now young adults, remember the lessons I tried to convey—such as, "Use what you have," and, "It doesn't matter how big or small your house is."

After I presented a few of the photographs to Devereaux's class, I realized the story of the Skinny House was more than a simple children's tale. It was, and is, an American parable that embodies values that we all cherish, such as hard work, optimism, and creativity. But it is also a story balanced with disaster, humiliation, and conflicts between parents and children. While the characters in this story and the events that affected them may not be familiar to all of us, they do raise universal questions about the reality, or myth as some may see it, of the inherent resilience of being human.

2

AMBIDEXTROUS

Nathan Seely

I NEVER MET MY GRANDFATHER Nathan. He died when I was seven years old. I heard bits and pieces about the man from anecdotes and stories my mother shared with us over the years. I knew that Nathan loved to build things and wanted to be his own boss. He loved the sound of a hammer striking wood, was mesmerized by the buzz of a saw, and reveled in the mess of sawdust. He measured everything in his life with the precision of a T-square ruler. He was of average height and build, but his large, rough hands, although rarely manicured, deftly drafted meticulous lists with the nub of a pencil he kept tucked behind one ear. He was a classy man who rarely wore a suit and instead preferred construction overalls, more often than not covered with a barely perceptible layer of dust and dirt. He loved classical music, and in later years would not turn off his truck radio until the last note of the final movement of the concerto was finished. He never traveled outside of the United States, but he was a worldly man. He spoke conversational Italian, used big words, and actually knew what they meant.

As I went about exploring more of his life story, I tried to nestle myself into every curve of his elegant calligraphy. Even in the most mundane of documents—his work ledger, the lists he kept, or an inscription on the back of a photograph—I sensed a man who tried to shout, "I am different! I can work and I will succeed!"

On a 1942 World War II draft record,[2] Nathan was asked to list his place of employment. He placed an asterisk next to the question to make the point that *he works for himself but hires out to contractors.* The phrase *works for himself* defined his character, because in his mind he was always in charge, a philosophy my grandmother and father, it seems, both came to resent.

There is another fact about Nathan that has always fascinated me. He was ambidextrous. I had to look up that word in the dictionary when I was in elementary school because it seemed to be such a complex word with different meanings. *Webster's Common Dictionary* defines the word as "using both hands with equal ease."[3] Scientists say that true ambidexterity affects only one percent of people, and Nathan was one of the rare ones. He never hesitated to show off his unusual skill by juggling apples, hammering a nail, or writing with both hands.

Nathan had no way of knowing that one day his ambidexterity would save his life. In 1958, while he was driving alone in his truck, he felt a sudden onset of weakness come over the right side of his body. One side of his face began to droop, and he started to drool and slur his words. A strange sensation crawled up one arm, rendering it numb and useless. Thanks to his ability to use both hands, he was able to steer the truck with his unaffected hand and pull over to the side of the road. He waited a few minutes and then managed to drive safely to the hospital. After the traumatic event, he described to my mother what sounded like all the classic symptoms of an evolving stroke.

Ambidextrous, I feel, also describes my grandfather's outlook on life. His brain seemed to be wired differently, and he often viewed the world and its challenges from a two-sided perspective. It seems to me that while he expressed his creativity in building things, he was at the same time trying to circumvent restrictions that he could not otherwise cross as a black man in the 1920s.

I have a few black-and-white photographs of Nathan. One stands out to me in particular. It is of him as a teenager, maybe seventeen or eighteen years old, around 1910, just about the time he left home for good to go out into the world. His gaze, slightly askew, seems to hang on the tail end of a joke. And judging by his smirk and centered cap, he felt himself in control of his life. He was a direct sort of guy, and perhaps a little bullheaded too. He was somewhat arrogant, or so I have heard. I like to think that what appeared to be arrogance in the 1900s was really the confidence a black boy needed to survive in those days, and to become a man, not to mention an entrepreneur.

My grandfather, Nathan Thomas Seely Sr., was born on February 24, 1893, in New Rochelle, New York. He was the oldest child of Charles G. Seely (born 1847) and Anna Morse Brooks (born 1862). Charles was labeled in the US Census records as a "mulatto[4]," a term derived from the Spanish-Portuguese word for *mule*, a hybrid between a horse and a donkey. The archaic and offensive description was used to describe the offspring of one black parent and one white parent.

Charles G. Seely, Nathan's father, undated.
Photo courtesy of Judy Seely

Charles was a handsome man with broad shoulders and a piercing gaze. He was not able to read or write, but he compensated for that handicap by working hard, first as a farm laborer and by 1905 as a night watchman. His lack of education did not stop him from eventually buying a home. He had two previous marriages and many children before marrying my great-grandmother Anna Brooks.

Anna, whose parents hailed from New York and North Carolina, was a very pretty woman with long, black hair that she piled up high on her head in a bun. She was a dressmaker by trade.

Charles and Anna made a striking couple. In 1892, they began their May–December marriage when Charles was fifty-two and Anna just twenty-nine years old. Anna bore eight children. Nathan's younger siblings included brothers Alonzo, Willard, Leon, Lester and sisters Edith, Mildred, Myrtle, and Anna. Another brother, Elroy, died at seven months of age. My uncle Willard and Nathan would later forge an inseparable bond as brothers and as business partners.

Nathan was just fourteen years old when his father died in 1906. Charles left no valid will, setting up circumstances in which his families, one in New York and one in New Jersey, pursued proceeds from a National City bank account. Seven hundred dollars was to be divided among more than a dozen children. It is not quite clear, but there also appeared to be $2,000 of "real property" that was "seized."[5]

After Charles's death, Anna was in dire straits. As a self-employed dressmaker, she had a meager income. I have no doubt Nathan felt an obligation to help his mother provide for the family. According to the 1910 US Census, Nathan, then seventeen years old, already listed himself as a carpenter. Seventeen was a common age for young men to leave school and begin an apprenticeship in a trade shop. The census documented that Nathan had finished one year of high school in New Rochelle. By 1912, he headed to Mamaroneck. I had no luck in finding details about his carpentry training in either New Rochelle or Mamaroneck.

However, by 1915, the Mamaroneck directory revealed that Nathan and his brother Willard lived in the same apartment house at 53 Grand Street. Nathan was working as a carpenter and Willard as a jockey. The abbreviation *col* appeared next to each of their names. At first I thought the abbreviation stood for colonel, but no, it stood for *colored*.

I am not sure where and when Nathan met my grandmother, but in October of 1915 he married Lillian Beatrice Booth at St. Luke's Episcopal Church in New Haven, Connecticut.

Lillian was born on April 5, 1895, in New Haven to George Frederick Booth (born 1865) and Edith Mae Bell (born 1874), a woman of Shinnecock Native American heritage. Lillian's father, originally from Long Island, was a Pullman porter for the railroad company. The history of this coveted job was significant not only because it employed many African-American men soon after the Civil War until 1968, but also because it helped spawn the growth of the black middle class in the United States. Working as a Pullman porter afforded blacks the opportunity to do things they had never done before—travel extensively and see how other folks lived.

Lillian Booth Seely,

undated 1915, ca age 21

The story goes that white industrialist George Pullman revolutionized the concept of sleeping car railroad service. After the Civil War, he hired former slaves to work as servants for well-to-do white passengers on long train trips. Many of the travelers were middle-class whites eager to experience the luxury of having a butler at their beck and call. While the black porters made their passengers' travel experiences enjoyable, their hours were long and exhausting. They were required to work at least 400 hours or 11,000 miles a month for deplorable base wages, and often with little sleep. They barely made a living on the tips they received, and they were penalized if any of their white patrons stole towels or supplies from the train. They were disrespected further because, as a rule, the white passengers called them all "George" and not by their real names. As journalist Thomas C. Fleming wrote in his series of *Reporter* newspaper articles in 1998, "Reflections on Black History," being a Pullman porter was "the best job in his (black) community and the worst on the train."[6]

It was not until 1925 that A. Philip Randolph—the same civil rights leader who proposed the 1941 and the actual 1963 March on Washington—formed the first black labor union, the Brotherhood of Sleeping Car Porters. The Pullman porters regained some dignity and respect from their employer and patrons after the formation of the union. This led to higher wages and, finally, official name badges to acknowledge who they were. If it were not for museums such as the A. Philip Randolph Pullman Porter Museum in Chicago and The Pullman Porter National Historic Registry[7] put together by historian Dr. Lyn Hughes, the details of this significant part of American history would be lost.

Given Lillian's family background, and after learning of the "hearsay" comments from her friends and acquaintances in New Haven, including my maternal West Indian–born grandmother, Dorothy Liburd Sargeant, I realized that my grandmother had aspired to marry a "professional" man as opposed to a man who did manual labor. Folks in New Haven were surprised Lillian married a carpenter, much less had two children. Like Nathan, she left school by the tenth grade and desperately wanted to escape the burden of caring for many younger siblings.

Lillian was just as determined a person as Nathan and just as ambitious for her family. She aspired to have a husband who would elevate her social status and provide her a higher standard of living. She wanted all the trappings of the black middle class: to become a housewife and focus on raising her own children instead of working as a domestic or in a factory. She wanted nice things such as an automobile and house. No doubt she recognized Nathan's potential as a husband, as well as his entrepreneurial skills and business acumen. Still, I wonder who courted whom.

By all accounts, Nathan adored Lillian, and he was determined to prove to her that he could provide a good life for her and their children. Around the time of their marriage, the United States was in the middle of World War I and had entered a period of innovation, especially in the fields of technology, manufacturing, and social activism. Thomas Edison had recently invented the Telescribe to record both sides of a telephone conversation. Alexander Graham Bell made the first transcontinental telephone call. Pyrex® dinnerware was invented. The Ford Motor Company manufactured its millionth Model T car. And Albert Einstein published his general theory of relativity.

White women and African-Americans broke barriers too. In 1916, Alice Paul formed the National Woman's Party and demanded a constitutional amendment for the right of women to vote. An African-American Harvard scholar, Dr. Carter B. Woodson, who would later create our modern-day Black History Month celebration each February, published the *Journal of Negro History* in 1915. Jack Johnson, the first black world heavyweight boxing champion, defended his title for the last time. The silent movie *The Birth of a Nation* by D. W. Griffith inspired the rebirth of the Ku Klux Klan in Georgia.

Nathan and Lillian settled in Mamaroneck just as World War I ended. Two years earlier they'd had their first child, a girl named Lillian Edith, whom they nicknamed "Sug," short for Sugar. Their son, Nathan Jr. nicknamed Tommy, was born in November of 1920. It was the beginning of the Roaring Twenties. Life was sweet.

My father "Tommy" and my Aunt " Sug" as toddlers. Undated, ca 1922 and 1920

3

WHERE THE SWEET WATERS FALL INTO THE SEA

Mamaroneck, New York, 1920s–1930s

MAMARONECK (ME-MAR-O-NEK). I HAVE LOVED that name forever. How can you not love a place at the mouth of the Sheldrake River, whose name, the locals say, popularly translates into "the place where the sweet waters fall into the sea or where the fresh waters fall into the salt"[8] There is a mystical sense of surrender and vulnerability in the description that reflects the story of the land purchase of Mamaroneck from Native Americans. In 1661, just three years before the Colony of New York was established, John Richbell, an English merchant and West Indies trader living in Oyster Bay, Long Island, bartered for three necks of land from Siwanoy Chief Wappaquewam and his brother, Mahatahan. He paid them not with precious coins, but with "two shirts and ten shillings in wampum, Twenty-two Coates [sic], one hundred fathom of wampum, Twelve shirts, Ten paire [sic] of Stockings, Twenty hands of powder, Twelve barrs of lead, Two firelockes, ffifteene [sic] Hoes, ffifteene [sic] Hatchets, and three Kettles."[9] The Indians lost Orienta, Larchmont Manor, and Premium Point. However, the transaction with Richbell did not stop them from selling two out of the same three necks of land a month later to another trader, Thomas Revell.[10] Richbell's claim to the land eventually held, setting the stage for a century and more of land transfers and property claims along the beautiful shores of the western Long Island Sound. Despite the transfer of land from one owner to another, and its passage from generation to generation, Mamaroneck perpetually drums its Native American heritage into my mind every time I utter its name, and I am drawn to this place where I did not grow up.

The Town of Mamaroneck, located in Westchester County about twenty-three miles from New York City, is subdivided into three sections: the Village of Larchmont, an unincorporated section, and the Village of Mamaroneck with its extension into the town of Rye.

The 1920 US Census listed many heads of households in Mamaroneck as first-generation Italian immigrants. These facts parallel the history of the development of suburbs in Westchester County. In the textbook *Westchester: The American Suburb*, editor Roger G. Panetta noted that George Lundberg, a professor of sociology at Columbia University, in 1929 described Westchester County "with its prized location" as "the laboratory for the study of leisure in a prosperous American suburb." Lundberg suggested Westchester County as a whole was considered a desirable suburb where you could escape the rat race of the city, engage in leisurely activities, and raise your children in a safe, country-like, and picturesque setting. Lundberg classified Westchester County suburbs into distinct types. The first type encompassed the wealthy villages of Bronxville, Larchmont, Pelham Manor, Scarsdale, and Rye, where the majority of land was used for private residences for privileged whites who commuted to Manhattan for professional jobs. The villages of Yonkers, Mount Vernon, New Rochelle, White Plains, and Port Chester were another distinct type of suburb—larger, urban, and more congested—and attracted a mix of families who "aspired to wealthy and middle class status." In contrast, Lundberg described the villages of Mamaroneck, Hastings, North Tarrytown, Tuckahoe, and Dobbs Ferry as "poor residential suburbs," home to middle-class working families, "resembling a small independent city, with a mix of foreign and second-generation population and pockets of [African-Americans].[11]

Nathan's story takes place in the working-class suburb of the Village of Mamaroneck. According to Lundberg's research in 1934 and a review of the 1930 US Census, Mamaroneck was home to 11,766 residents, of whom 27 percent (3,175) were foreign-born whites, and only 3.9 percent (454) were Negroes.[12]

In spite of its proximity to the island of Manhattan and the bustling Metro-North Amtrak commuter railway line, there is still something peaceful about Mamaroneck. About half of this 6.7-square-mile area is covered by water. The water is so close that, if you stand at the center of the Village of Mamaroneck at the corner of Boston Post Road and Mamaroneck Avenue and then look over your shoulder toward the harbor, you can see rows of stick-straight sailboat masts bobbing like pistons on the dark waters that eventually flow into the sound. Walk a block toward the water and you can smell the tide and hear the clanking of the boat locks rocking gently on the waves.

Intimacy with the sea has its price, particularly in the Washingtonville section of Mamaroneck Village, nicknamed "The Flats" because of its low tidal basin. In this area, the Mamaroneck and Sheldrake rivers snake their way through the neighborhoods, their trails often invisible except for the perennial damp soil they leave behind. The tendency to flood in this low-lying area may help explain why Washingtonville was slow to develop in the late 1800s and never materialized as a middle-class railroad commuter suburb. It also may explain why the wealthy suburbanites at the time considered the land less desirable, and instead preferred to settle in the surrounding higher-elevated neighborhoods overlooking the harbor such as Heathcoat Hill. However, working-class people in the Village, many African-Americans and first-generation immigrants, recognized opportunities to buy land cheaply at county tax auctions, and thus they, too, became landowners.[13]

In the Washingtonville neighborhood on Grand Street where my grandparents settled in 1918, the fathers made their living as carpenters, masons, laborers, chauffeurs, porters, and servants. The mothers, especially the African-American mothers, could not afford the luxury of staying home to raise their children. They worked as domestic servants, cooks, and seamstresses in the surrounding homes of their wealthy neighbors.

The handful of black families who lived on Grand Street lived alongside first-generation Italian immigrant families from places such as Naples, Palermo, and Sicily. These black and white children played together and attended the same public schools by necessity, and their parents bought groceries on credit at the same corner grocery store.

On Grand Street just off Mamaroneck Avenue, neighborhood kids included those from the Tedeschi, Tomasetti, Santangelo, Brooks, Seely, and Rogers families. Their children played games of kickball with an old can, hopscotch, and hide-and-seek according to Ida Santangelo, a long-term resident.

At a Grand Street reunion in 1980, some of the kids, by then adults raising children of their own, recounted the good times they had.

"Oh, we had good old times," said Mrs. Santangelo. "We were poor, but we shared what we had. My mother used to bake bread and pass it around to all of us. And we were black and we were white and it didn't make a difference.[14]

The grandmothers of the extended Italian families, many of whom spoke only broken English, would chase any loose child up and down the street, shouting in Italian, "You eat! *Tu mangi!*" Once they caught a little rascal, they would spoon-feed him or her macaroni, beans, or on special occasions, a raw egg concoction from "the old country" deemed good for their health.

The men played bocce ball. Every September, the aroma of homemade wine signaled the harvest of grapes, not from some grand, fancy vineyard but from the simple, yet bountiful, grape arbors that lined many front yards.

In addition to working-class families, Mamaroneck attracted its fair share of famous citizens over the decades. James Fenimore Cooper, author of the classic tale *The Last of the Mohicans*, was married in the Delancey

Mansion on Heathcote Hill. Ethel Barrymore, the stage and movie actress of the 1950s, lived on Taylor Lane, and Norman Rockwell, the famous portrait illustrator, attended Mamaroneck High School before heading to Chase Art School in New York City.

My working-class and famous grandfather settled in the Village soon after he was married.

4

HOMES FOR COLORED PEOPLE

The Seely Bros. Company, Purpose and Mission

O———⚓

"Every colored man needs a home. That statement does not require proof. It is the dearest wish of every individual of every color or race to have a clean, decent place in which to house his family, in which to bring up his children in peace and comfort."

—Seely Bros., Inc. brochure, circa 1925

IN 1920, NATHAN WAS TWENTY-EIGHT years old. Family records show he and Lillian obtained a $100 loan from the First National Bank of Mamaroneck suggesting he was credit-worthy and had steady income as a self-employed carpenter. I was unable to find out whether he was a member of the United Brotherhood of Carpenters (UBC), and Joiners of America Union, a national labor federation for carpenters started in 1881 that had proposed from its inception to admit both black and white carpenters. The union sought to strengthen collective bargaining, and to promote an eight-hour workday, fair pay, and benefits for workers in the building trades. One of the founders of the UBC, Peter J. McGuire, was responsible for creating the national Labor Day holiday.

A Seely work ledger from 1921 revealed that Nathan worked six eight-hour days each week and charged $1.25 per hour, a decent amount above the $1.00 average hourly wage for the building trades in the United States at the time.[15] In 1920, $1.00 had the same buying power as $11.93 today.[16] On several jobs he paid his brother Willard, a laborer at a lumberyard, eighty-seven cents per hour to assist him.

My Great-Uncle Willard, Nathan's business partner.
Obituary photograph 1984.

I know very little about Uncle Willard, but according to the Westchester County land records, he was the first Seely brother to become a landowner. Like Nathan, he loved to work with his hands, so much so that he continued to work as a landscape gardener at age ninety. He met, fell in love, and married Alvina Gudger in 1940, a Mamaroneck resident who took in boarders during the early years of the Depression. While Willard had no children of his own, he inherited stepsons and relocated with his new family to California several years after Seely Bros., Inc. folded. He died there in 1984.

Willard's obituary notice included a version of a famous quotation attributed to the Hollywood actress Mary Pickford: "The past cannot be changed. The future is yet in your power." Added to the quotation was, "With God, nothing is impossible." It seems to me those statements reflected

Willard's faith and inherent belief in self-preservation and in leading a proactive and ambitious life.

In Mamaroneck Village in early 1920, Nathan and Willard developed reputations as dependable local contractors. Nathan initially took on small jobs, such as installing or repairing screens, hanging doors, repairing roofs, and building flower boxes for well-to-do clients in Larchmont and Heathcote Hill. He soon moved on to completing more demanding projects, such as building terraces and garages, for which he supervised a crew of subcontracted laborers.

I found references in one work ledger that Nathan loaned out his motorcar for money. It was no surprise to me that he wanted another source of income besides contracting work—understandable given his personal circumstances. Lillian was pregnant at the time, plus he needed seed money to start his own business.

By 1922, the abbreviation *col* had thankfully disappeared next to Nathan's listing in the local village directory. He was listed as the first director at a New Rochelle construction company doing business as Richardson Realty. The other investors included a physician, a cabinetmaker, a carpenter, and a furniture dealer. All of these men were first-generation immigrants or American participants in the Great Migration. All appeared to be hardworking, forward-thinking men like Nathan.

At the time of incorporation, Richardson Realty had capital stock of $25,000, and for the next ten years it focused on leasing apartments and had a goal to build two-family homes.[17]

In Mamaroneck Village, the deed records show that Willard began to purchase land as early as 1920.[18] According to a 1923 newspaper announcement, Willard and Nathan jointly purchased Lots 203 and 205 on Warren Street from an owner named Mary Foley. On this site they built a three-family apartment house.[19] When they flipped a dilapidated house and renovated it into a duplex home, the new owners were each given an engraved Seely Bros. key as a house-warming gift.

Nathan and Willard purchased another four lots of land that year, this time from the estate of Maria Denison and her husband Eugene, first-generation immigrants from France. The four-lot section included Lots 194, 196, 198, and 200.[20] The Skinny House would later be built on a portion of Lot 196.

Around this time, the brothers began to strategize about starting their own company. They probably sensed it was a propitious time to invest in a business because the United States was in a construction boom. The estimated number of national employees in the construction industry rose from 932,000 in 1920 to 1.5 million by 1925.[21]

Seely Bros. was incorporated on April 18, 1925.[22] The corporation filing listed other directors besides Nathan and Willard, three of whom were African-American businessmen living in the White Plains area. Mr. Arthur R. Davis worked in real estate and was an immigrant from the British West Indies. Rev. W. H. Edwin Smith founded the Second Baptist Church in White Plains and later relocated to New Hampshire, where he became the first black moderator for a Baptist Church organization. Mr. James A. Blythe was a cook and an immigrant from Jamaica. Mrs. Lillian E. Shapiro was listed as acting secretary. The last and most prominent director was Oscar LeRoy Warren, a local attorney who worked in the county clerk's office. I came upon Mr. Warren's name often in the Village of Mamaroneck land records. As the court clerk, he officiated over many land transfers. His name came up again in 1933 when his criminal activities became front-page news and his personal character came into question.

I wanted to find out more about what motivated two African-American brothers to become entrepreneurs in the early 1920s. What did they think they had going for them? Wasn't this a bold move for black men at the time?

To understand the times, I had to revisit the era of the Roaring Twenties. World War I had ended in 1918, a deadly tide of influenza had been extinguished, and the United States was transitioning into a peacetime economy. People were moving away from rural areas and farms and relocating to major cities such as New York and Chicago, where they could earn more as factory workers or take other industrial jobs. It was possible to earn five dollars a day—maybe not as much as that if you were a black man, but if you wanted to work, jobs were available. The US unemployment rate for 1922–1923 was estimated to be barely 5–7 percent, depending upon the source of the data and the particular industry.[23] Strong consumer demand for goods and housing led to exponential growth in the building and technology industries. Industry profits and construction were robust. The well-to-do folks drove their new Ford Model T cars, and equipped their homes with electricity and telephones. Going to a motion picture show became a favorite pastime. People actually had time for leisure activities.

In the early 1920s on the artistic front, the Art Deco era commenced, and the Jazz Age sauntered in, paving the way for trumpeter Louis Armstrong, pianist Duke Ellington, and singer Bessie Smith, among others, to showcase their musical talents to the world through this new gadget called a radio. Broadway's George Gershwin and Cole Porter wrote songs and lyrics that were timely and became timeless. Author William Faulkner wrote haunting, vivid stories about poor folks, while F. Scott Fitzgerald wrote about the playgrounds of rich white people. The Harlem Renaissance ushered in the vivid cultural poetry of Langston Hughes. Carl Sandburg's poetry danced off the pages and into the hearts of Americans.

White women found a new voice in 1926 too, and decided they could wear shorter dresses with dropped waistlines, they could wear makeup, and they could smoke if they wanted. They tried to prove they had the bravado to drink as much as any man. The "flapper" epitomized the "modern" woman, one who loved to dance, who made her own decisions, and even had the audacity to want to vote.

The societal freedom that the Roaring Twenties ushered in was tempered, literally, by a few other pivotal social movements, the first being Prohibition, an Eighteenth Amendment ban on the sale, production, importation, and transportation of alcoholic beverages in the United States that started at midnight on January 17, 1920. The ban was broken within its first hour of implementation, and lasted until December 6, 1933, the year after Nathan moved his family into the Skinny House. Prohibition brought about the demise of "men only" saloons, gave rise to equal opportunity illegal speakeasies—bars disguised as flower shops—and fueled the growth of organized crime, mobsters, and bootlegging. Surprisingly, the women's suffrage movement, according to historian-editor Daniel Okrent, was closely entwined with temperance and supported Prohibition.[24]

Secondly, the Roaring Twenties era was tempered by an anti-immigration sentiment, fueled mostly by white rural Protestants who felt threatened by the influx of immigrants into the urban cities.

And lastly, for most African-Americans who still lived in the Deep south,[25] the Roaring Twenties were anything but an era of societal freedom. Jim Crow laws were in full force and membership in the Ku Klux Klan peaked in the 1920s.

I surmise the newly found societal freedom of the Roaring Twenties influenced Nathan and Willard. The brothers began to think anything was possible. They envisioned a more modern lifestyle and culture. Like many northern African-Americans, they sensed an opportunity to break from tradition and to actually become middle-class American citizens. Why not dream of starting a construction company? Why not take part in the Harlem Renaissance movement in a unique way?

Nathan and Willard had the good fortune of being African-American men who lived in a village only a short train ride from the modern metropolis of New York City, where there appeared to be more tolerance and equitable economic opportunities for minorities as compared to the southern states. Their business goals were bolstered by the intellectual mecca of Harlem, where a myriad of black authors, poets, actors, and musicians inspired dreams, opened doors, and hammered racist stereotypes with their pens, paintings, plays, and prose.

In fact, I believe the evolution of the Harlem Renaissance from 1918 through the mid-1930s, which occurred in an urban borough of Manhattan just a train ride away from Mamaroneck, combined with the Great Migration of blacks from the Deep south to the North, were the two major cultural influences on Nathan and his brother Willard as young men dreaming to take control of their lives.

The Harlem Renaissance was a "cultural, social, and artistic[26]" movement begun by American blacks, but it attracted and welcomed blacks from the Caribbean, black expatriates from Europe, and many African nations.

The borough of Harlem might have originated as a destination for affluent whites, but by the late nineteenth century, European immigrants had established a significant residence. World War I ended and set the stage for the trickle of immigrants into the country and the simultaneous influx of southern American blacks to New York. Harlem's black population swelled in the 1920s in response to the same demand for unskilled industrial labor that fueled the migration of people in rural areas to urban centers.

Nathan knew that, although he would not escape racism in Mamaroneck, his experience living there was drastically better than that of a black man living in the Deep south. He was afforded opportunities for education and advancement not available to many southern blacks. What else motivated him?

In my research, I discovered another possible source of inspiration for Nathan and Willard. Nathan subscribed to *The Crisis* magazine, the flagship publication of the civil rights organization founded in 1909 called the National Association for the Advancement of Colored People, otherwise known as the NAACP. The magazine's first editor was

NAACP co-founder, Dr. W. E. B. DuBois, an activist, author, Harvard sociologist, and scholar. The publication's subtitle was *A Record of the Darker Races*, and its articles tapped the pulse of educated African-Americans, particularly those on the East Coast who were discussing and debating issues of civil rights openly in print. In particular, during the 1915–1916 years when Nathan and Lillian were newlyweds eager to work their way up the middle-class ladder, the magazine regularly covered two civil rights topics in great detail: the denouncement of lynching in the south and support of the Great Migration of southern blacks to the northeastern, western, and Midwestern United States.[27] By 1920, DuBois used more direct language to encourage blacks to leave the south and titled his editorial, "Brothers, Come North."[28]

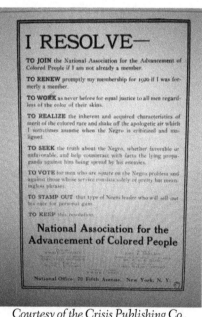

The Crisis Magazine January 1920 Cover and I RESOLVE NAACP CREDO. Courtesy of the Crisis Publishing Co., Inc., the publisher of the magazine of the National Association for the Advancement of Colored People.

Courtesy of the Crisis Publishing Co., Inc., the publisher of the magazine of the National Association for the Advancement of Colored People. Cover Vol. 19-No.3, Jan 1920: Woman of Santa Lucia, Photograph by Brown & Dawson

The Crisis magazine also served as a literary journal for poets and authors of the Harlem Renaissance such as Countee Cullen, nee Coleman Rutherford, and Langston Hughes. However, the magazine's main goal was to spotlight the civil injustices imposed upon blacks. The March 1926 issue, which would have come out just before Seely Bros., Inc. launched, celebrated one of the most successful years for the NAACP, and outlined one of the most crucial issues of the day for blacks: the problem of residential segregation and discrimination.[29]

The NAACP also noted that discriminatory strategies implemented at the time included designing property-holder covenants to prevent transfer of property to blacks, and inciting mob violence against black homebuyers. Other strategies blatantly proposed legislation restricting blacks to live in certain areas. Detroit at the time was the poster city for these kinds of discriminatory practices. The city was inundated with poor blacks migrating from Arkansas, Alabama, Louisiana, and Mississippi, and the newcomers were competing with their poor white counterparts for jobs. The stage was set for a serious, explosive housing shortage.

The Seely brothers decided their contribution, as responsible men of color, would be to help alleviate the housing shortage for African-American families migrating to Mamaroneck. They sought to provide families an opportunity to rent a decent apartment, to own a home, and even to invest in a black-owned business. These families, often arriving from Virginia, the Carolinas, Georgia, and Florida, came in search of jobs. Many of the newly arriving workers were women who had left their families behind to take servant positions in the homes of wealthy families living in Rye and Larchmont. These "sleep-in" maids, as they were called, worked five to six days a week, and if their employer did not supply room and board, they had few options for a place to stay on their day off—if they got a day off. Often, two to three maids would pool their earnings in order to afford to rent an apartment.[30]

Nathan addressed these issues directly in the Seely Bros., Inc. mission statement:

> There has been a great increase in recent years in the colored population of the North. This has brought with it a very serious housing problem. No longer is it easy for the colored man to find, at the price he can afford to pay, a decent place in which to live. Nor can he look to the white man for assistance. That individual is too busy making a living for his own family to worry about the difficulties of any race. The colored people must work out their own problems; they must help each other. It is for that great purpose that Seely Brothers, Inc., has been organized. It will supply colored people everywhere with homes.

The families Nathan and Willard desired to help were like those described in Isabel Wilkerson's book *The Warmth of Other Suns*,[31] a compilation of personal stories of blacks taking part in the Great Migration from the south to the Midwest.

Nathan and Willard designed the *Homes for Colored People* brochure not only to outline their mission but also to rally the black community into becoming investors. The stock prospectus's tone was simple and direct:

> Part of the preferred stock of the company is now being offered for sale to a select list of colored people. It sells for $10 per share and pays interest at the rate of 8% per year, twice that paid by a savings bank. In addition to this, with each share of preferred stock will be given free a share of common stock of the par value of $5 per share. Among holders of this common stock will be divided all the additional earnings of the company. These should be very large.

The optimistic tone continued:

Don't you want to join with the other men whose names have been given in this booklet and aid in great work? Remember, if you do, you will be sure of two things:

First, you will greatly aid your own colored race by supplying homes. Secondly, you will make money for yourself.

Short-term and long-term business goals of the company included the following:

Apartment houses, stores, lodge rooms, amusement halls, one and two family homes will be erected or bought. Tracts of land will be bought and divided into building lots. These properties will be rented and sold, bringing in revenue to the company.

Nathan was the ultimate pitchman in 1925. In essence, he was saying: *This is our story; these are our goals, and for your loyalty and support, you will be a part of the new generation of forward-thinking African-Americans.* The confident tone of the brochure is consistent with what I know of Nathan's personality. You can feel his excitement and hope for the future. He believed in his own abilities, he believed in his brother Willard's partnership, and he believed in his potential investors. Most of all, he wanted his investors to know, as he says in the brochure, that he and Willard had attained success through honesty and hard work and that they had earned the position of being substantial citizens of the community, without regard to race or color.

Nathan, Willard and an unidentified man
on the porch of a Seely Bros. house, June 1923

The company office was located at 95 S. Lexington Avenue in White Plains, where today the White Plains Galleria Mall and state government buildings claim the neighborhood. It was one of the first African-American-owned construction companies in New York.

By the time the company was incorporated, Nathan and Willard had secured loans and purchased "everything they needed to do their work cheaply and efficiently—including labor-saving machinery," such as trucks, tractors, power-driven saws, and woodworking machinery. Most of the company's machinery and equipment was stored at construction worksites, but Nathan also built a large company toolshed on his private

C. G. Seely Apartment Building, 1923

property, the narrow lot where eventually the Skinny House would be built. A portion of this toolshed would later be recycled and incorporated into the frame of the Skinny House. The company was also prosperous enough to hire skilled laborers, such as masons, roofers, and electricians. At the height of its success, the company operated six Mack trucks and had its own secretary and attorney.

Nathan continued to be proactive about taking his skill sets to the next level. He enrolled in a night class to learn how to draft blueprints. Clearly he believed in setting goals and mapping out a route to success. He had his own internal, well-calibrated GPS, but the economic collapse of the 1930s was just ahead on a treacherous road. Despite numerous attempts to "recalculate" his route and to circumvent roadblocks, Nathan confronted a major obstacle, the Great Depression. For a short, sweet time, however, he and Willard had their feet firmly planted on the road to success.

5

Good Times

Custom Built Middle Class Dreams

Lillian, in front of the custom home
Nathan built for her in 1926-1927

By July of 1926, Nathan had designed and built a grand house for Lillian on Lot 194, now 173 Grand Street. I still get a kick out of reading the document titled *Specifications for a Residence to Be Erected at Mamaroneck, New York for Mrs. Lillian B. Seely*.[32] To me, the title alone signifies Nathan's love and respect for my grandmother.

Nathan was no typical owner–builder. Every detail mattered to him. The specifications for Lillian's house, including the utilities and interior finishes, were remarkable. The document emphasized the use of high-quality materials and the meticulous workmanship he expected. For instance:

> All materials, labor, and mechanical appliances shall be first class unless especially mentioned otherwise. All timber is to be of sound, well-seasoned spruce. All the entire outside finish must be well-seasoned cypress free from large and loose knots. The finished floors in the hall, living room, and dining room are to be oak parquet with a border of two walnut stripes. The hardware of the interior doors will include cut-glass knobs with screw-type spindles.

The most innovative feature of the Seelys' grand home was the installation of indoor plumbing, an uncommon convenience for much of the housing industry in 1926. Unless they were wealthy, most families used outhouses, a one-room wooden shack separated from the main house that was built over a pit in the ground. Imagine using a windowless outhouse on a hot summer evening. As children of one of the first families on Grand Street with indoor plumbing, Tom and Suge, throughout their childhood, had the luxury of using a private bathroom.

Another innovative feature of Nathan's customized home included a central heating system. According to the building specifications, the hot water boiler had to be:

> Sufficiently large enough to heat the entire house, including garage, to a temperature of 70 degrees Fahrenheit, when the temperature outside is zero...The heating contractor must submit guarantee for his work for a period of one year from date of completion and every part of the work must be done in the best workman-like manner.

Nathan held his subcontractors to high standards, so it was not surprising that he would later build the Skinny House with the same attention to detail, custom features, and quality materials—perhaps salvaged materials, but high quality nonetheless.

In my eyes, the specifications for the first family home on Grand Street were a reflection of Nathan's creativity. Lillian considered the house her pride and joy. In one photograph taken in front of the house, she poses with one hand propped on her hip and the other one artfully concealing a cigarette. She had finally arrived and was a *modern woman* of America's middle class. She was the queen of her household and she had a beautiful home to prove it. She intended to live in her grand house forever.

During the profitable years of his company, Nathan drove a Hudson Super-Six car. It was a classy blue-and-black motor coach that had to be ordered directly from the factory in Detroit. At the time, the cost was $1,200 to $1,700 and, depending on the model, seated a family of four to seven people.

1924 Magazine Ad for Hudson
Motor Cars Coach Super-Six Vehicle,
Courtesy of FCA US LLC

Although Lillian knew how to drive, she never drove the Hudson, but she enjoyed the attention this status symbol garnered. She especially loved the electric horn that announced their arrival or, I imagine, warned people to get the hell out of their way! According to my father's account, Lillian routinely scolded Nathan whenever she caught him driving the Hudson while wearing his dirty construction overalls.

On occasional Sunday afternoons, dressed in her Sunday best, Lillian insisted Nathan drive the family into Harlem. Nathan dressed up too, but in clean overalls, despite my grandmother's protest. According to my mother, Nathan was wary of folks dressed up in fancy clothes. He was who he was, a hardworking carpenter who judged people by their character and not by the clothes they wore.

Once in Harlem, Lillian instructed Nathan to park the Hudson in front of the great Abyssinian Baptist Church so she could watch other middle-class black churchgoers strut in their Sunday best outfits. This people-watching pastime was likely my grandmother's idea, but I surmise my grandfather enjoyed it too, as he admired the political and social activism the well-known pastor, Rev. Adam Clayton Powell Sr., and his family championed. The pastor's son, the Rev. Adam Clayton Powell Jr., became a noted civil rights leader in the 1930s. He crusaded for jobs and affordable housing for the poor and became the first African-American congressman from New York. In 1961, he acted as the chairman of the influential Education and Labor Committee that legislated crucial minimum-wage bills and a plethora of social and educational reforms.

Nathan and Lillian had all the trappings of success in the early 1920s. They owned a beautiful home, drove a fancy motor coach, ran a highly reputable construction business, and owned real estate. They were living the American dream. Every night, just before the family sat down to eat, my grandfather would proclaim, "Now, let's have a nice get-together." To me, his expression translates today into something like: *Every family dinner is special, and we should not take our time together for granted.*

My father is the boy wearing a tie in the center of the back row in this kindergarten photo.

Unknown photographer. ca 1925.

Aunt Sug, age 12, and my father, age 9, ca. 1930

Nathan and Lillian were grateful for their good times in more ways than one.

Sug and Tom attended public schools throughout kindergarten, junior high, and high school. I was surprised to learn that in the 1920s, the Mamaroneck Village public classrooms were integrated. Tom's kindergarten class had eighteen children, three of whom were black. He reaped the benefits of attending a northern school that had more financial resources, smaller classes, and more highly trained teachers than those in a segregated school in the south.

The institution of racism, however, did not skip over the village, but it was not until Tom entered the Army in 1941 as a young adult that he

Boy Scout Troop 7, est. at the Barry Avenue A. M. E. Church. My father Tommy is the first boy on the right standing in the third row. June 15, 1935. Photographer is unknown.

would experience blatant segregation and racism for the first time. He and other African-American young men, especially from the New England area, would be drafted into World War II and shipped to segregated boot camps.

Despite the large number of immigrants in the Village of Mamaroneck at the time, first-generation Italian Americans were also targets of prejudice. Ninety-one-year-old Mamaroneck resident Ida Santangelo, daughter of Mr. Panfilo Santangelo, Nathan's neighbor, recalled as a child being labeled a "little Spic" just because her parents spoke English as a second language.

Nathan and Lillian were one of many African-American families in the Village of Mamaroneck who created their own strong sense of community, often centered on the church.

Lillian attended the Barry Avenue African Methodist Episcopal (AME) Zion Church, located a short distance from Grand Street. The landmark house of worship was founded by a runaway slave from Louisiana named Robert Purdy, who was instrumental in turning the church into a safe haven for the Underground Railroad.

The church congregation established the first African-American Boy Scout troop in the Mamaroneck district, named the Flying Eagle Patrol of Troop 7. Tom was patrol leader in 1935, and that year his team won the Interpatrol Championship Rally, where they showcased knot tying, first aid, and Morse code signaling. Their prizes were ice cream cones. Troop 7 was such an integral part of the African-American community in Mamaroneck Village that, even today, if you were to ask a black baby-boomer resident about it, they could likely point out a grandfather, father, or an uncle in the same photograph in which Tom's deadpan adolescent face stared into the camera.

My father was a lanky adolescent with freckles and flaming carrot-topped hair. He was shy and studious, and often had his head buried in a book. In contrast, my Aunt Sug was very outgoing and personable. It is easy to understand why she became popular in school with her flawless caramel skin, long black braids, and dark, piercing eyes. While Tom was participating in the Boy Scouts, Sug was winning prizes for her singing. A 1935 article in the *New York Age* newspaper announced that Nathan and Tom had accompanied her to New Rochelle in order to hear her perform.

As siblings, Sug and Tom were very close. They called each other "Sonny" and "Sis." Sug was Tom's number one fan, and she adored her brother. Throughout the course of Tom's lifetime, she would chronicle his achievements, awards, and accolades, and bind them in large, fancy scrapbooks. Thanks to her love of scrapbooking, I discovered many details about their relationship and my father's career path. Tom, in turn, was fiercely protective of his sister, and even as he grew older, he made no apologies for voicing his opinion to her about her personal life, whether she welcomed it or not.

Nathan and Lillian were sticklers for education and musical training. Every day, Sug and Tommy had to choose five words from the dictionary, learn how to spell them, and use each one in a sentence. Lillian was the music teacher in the household. She cherished their upright piano so much that to her, it was a member of the family. She taught Tom how to play the piano long before the violin became his official instrument in school, and she enrolled Sug in the church choir, where her love of singing was born.

Changing Times

6

Descent

Desperation and the Great Depression

The Brooklyn Daily Eagle. October 24, 1929. Getty Images.

ON TUESDAY, OCTOBER 29, 1929, better known as Black Tuesday, the Dow Jones Industrial Average fell some thirty points and lost nearly $14 billion in a single day. The tanking of the stock market ushered in the beginning of one of the darkest decades in American history, the Great Depression.

There are many theories about which economic events caused what circumstances that led to the Great Depression. Some blame the emigration of families from rural areas into the industrial cities that left

American farmers unable to make a living and unable to pay their debts or mortgages, thus triggering the first wave of an agricultural financial depression.[33] Another respected explanation is Irving Fisher's debt-deflation theory.[34] Fisher argued that excessive debt led to a chain reaction of financial events that included, among others, distress selling, a decrease in construction, the failure of banks, and ultimately pessimism and lack of consumer confidence in the market.

Indeed, toward the end of the Roaring Twenties, US banks were willing to lend nine dollars for every dollar an investor deposited.[35] Bank loans on credit were easy to obtain, but when the market fell, the banks called in these loans, which could not be paid back. With little supply of money, debtors such as my grandfather and uncle defaulted on their business loans. American depositors withdrew their deposits en masse, and bank failures snowballed. Capital investment and the construction of homes, the lifeline income for my grandfather, came to an abrupt halt.

Nick Taylor sums up the era of the Great Depression succinctly in his 2008 book *American Made: The History of the Works Progress Administration*. He opens the prologue of his book with this statement: "The human toll of the Great Depression of the 1930s is almost impossible for us to fathom.[36]" The first chapter is pretty gut-wrenching. It is titled "The End of Jobs," referring particularly to 1932, the year the Dow Jones Industrial Average hit its lowest point and the same year my grandparents, Tom, and Sug moved into the Skinny House.

Nathan was a driven man who found himself in a desperate situation. He was thirty-six years old when the stock market crashed, but it is clear from land records that he was in severe financial trouble as early as 1927. I think he quickly realized he was in trouble because there had been a dramatic slowing of national steel production and local construction projects. His borrowing and credit were impacted, and subsequently, interest rates on his loans rose exorbitantly. He was highly leveraged and had little cash reserve, having poured all of the initial profits back into the company. The net worth of Seely Bros., Inc. plummeted. The business was sucked up into the vortex of the Depression, and as with thousands of Americans, Nathan's and Willard's dreams as entrepreneurs were pulverized and spit out like nasty chewing gum.

Nathan's and Willard's financial crises were reflected in a series of land transfers recorded in the Westchester County land records from 1927 through 1935. Much of the land they had purchased was mortgaged to the hilt, and by the summer of 1927, they were unable to make payments toward these debts.

On May 10, 1927, the company was forced to sell the first portion of Lot 203 on Grand Street, where they had built an apartment house. County records show a mortgage debt of $7,200.[37] The property was sold to Rita Rodney, and that portion of land passed out of our family. One month later, the company foreclosed on the other portion of Lot 203 and Lot 205. These sales were to Phillip H. Seaman and A. U. Rodney, Inc.[38]

There were other clues that Nathan and Willard were in financial trouble. Just six days prior to the US stock market "mini-crash" on March 12, 1929, Nathan's mother transferred property originally owned by Willard to attorney and company investor, Oscar LeRoy Warren.[39] On the same day in 1929, Westchester County land records revealed that Nathan, Willard, and Lillian, as guarantors, sold Lot 198, the easterly 37.5 feet of lot 202 and a large portion of Lot 196 to Warren. The deed between Seely and Warren had typing errors that resulted in a mistaken description of the metes and bounds. The errors were never corrected, but it was clear that the 12.5-foot portion of Lot 196, where the Skinny House would later be built in 1932, was excluded from the land sales to Warren. Later that year, on August 8, 1929, Mr. Warren sold the lots he had purchased to Panfilo and Maria Santangelo.[40] The deed records also do not support the newspaper claims over the years that Mr. Santangelo purchased Nathan's former land and gifted him the narrow strip of land back for $1 to build the Skinny House. I was unable to find a purchase or donation agreement between Mr. Santangelo and Nathan. Instead, the records support Lillian's refrain that my mother had heard throughout her marriage, that the Skinny House was built on a narrow strip of land that was "free and clear," and that Nathan, Willard, and Lillian, having originally purchased the Skinny House lot as part of the original Marie Denison estate in 1923, together remained owners of the lot until the two brothers transferred sole ownership to Lillian in 1949.

Had there been a gentleman's agreement between Mr. Santangelo and Nathan to the effect that he would donate the Skinny House lot back to Nathan? Possibly. Mr. Santangelo may have believed the Skinny House lot was included in his purchase from Warren. However, it is just as possible that Nathan demanded the 12.5' x 100' Skinny House lot be excluded from the Warren transaction so he could build a home for his family. In my opinion, the latter decision is in line with Nathan's personality and his self-reliance goals as outlined in the Homes for Colored People brochure. One thing is for sure: the untrustworthy participant in the real estate transaction was Mr. Warren. It would have been to his advantage to make the sale and to have Mr. Santangelo and Nathan feel like they were both winners.

The 1930 US Census revealed Nathan, listed as a builder, had been on the unemployment rolls for more than two years. When you're sucker punched, the blow is extra devastating because you have little time to defend yourself, to block the blow, or even to duck. Nathan was no sucker by all accounts, and he was not a man easily deceived. I think he probably knew the direction his company was headed as early as 1927, but perhaps he misjudged the swiftness of its descent and the impact on his family. I can only imagine the sense of devastation this hardworking man must have felt. His good life was slowly turning into a nightmare. There were more challenges to come.

No matter how shocked he may have been, Nathan was a proud man who would have forestalled telling Lillian the bad news. Lillian was an astute woman and wise enough to know that many families were in the same boat. She probably counted herself fortunate to have a husband who had a skill, and was a partner who would be able to take care of her, Sug, and Tom. Still, my grandmother did not take the news well. Her fears were allayed for a short time when Nathan managed to scrape together enough money to keep them in their home until May 1930, but soon the bank foreclosed on their mortgage. Now Nathan had to scramble and figure out a way to keep a roof over their heads.

Why did the Seely family lose their original 1926 grand home Nathan had built for Lillian on Lot 194 while some families on Grand Street managed to keep their homes? There may have been several reasons. Lillian owned her grand house "free and clear" when Nathan transferred Lot 194 to her in October 1926.[41] However, in February 1927, she took out a mortgage on the property with the Railroad Cooperative Building and Loan Association.[42] By May 1930, the loan association had foreclosed on the property.[43] I have to wonder whether, if not for that mortgage, perhaps Lillian and Nathan could have kept their home. Did Lillian take out the mortgage on her grand house to bail Nathan out of the Seely Bros., Inc. business debts?

I surmise there might be another reason Nathan and Lillian fared poorly compared to others on Grand Street. The family had only one source of income, Nathan's, and as an entrepreneur with mounting debts, it was not a steady income. In contrast, many immigrant families lived together as large extended families in single households and some even took on boarders who could help pay the mortgage. These families pooled whatever meager financial resources they had in order to pay their debts. Sometimes even that was not enough. Mr. Santangelo, Nathan's next-door neighbor for some fifty years, was the patriarch of one of those families. His daughter, Ida Santangelo, recalled that in 1940, the bank foreclosed on their house, and had it not been for a close family friend who came to their rescue, they too would have lost their home in those dire circumstances.[44]

While some families survived the devastation of the Depression due to their pooled family resources or a generous benefactor, Nathan was not so fortunate. He and Willard were unsuccessful in calling in their invoices. They simply had no funds to pay their creditors. Willard went to live at a local boarding house in order to make ends meet.

Lastly, and most importantly, the severe economic devastation of the Depression affected the most vulnerable population first: namely, African-Americans who were subjected to segregation and racism when it came to employment, regardless of whether they were skilled men or not. Cheryl Lynn Greenberg's 2010 book *To Ask for an Equal Chance* states that, "even before 1929, the vast majority [of blacks] lived in desperate poverty" and during the Depression, they were the "last hired, first fired."[45]

In Mamaroneck, the consequences of the Depression were severe and swift. According to the Town of Mamaroneck's website, there were so many home foreclosures that the town imposed a ban on placing "For Sale" signs on front lawns for fear of panic.

When Nathan's custom-built family home at 37 Grand Street went into foreclosure, he had to think quickly. He realized that the large company toolshed on the narrow 12.5' x 100' lot next to their house could serve as a temporary storage place for some of the family's personal possessions and company tools until he could get back on his feet.

Nathan spared Lillian, Tom, and Sug the shame of moving out of their custom-built home and immediately sent them away to live with Lillian's family in New Haven. It is certainly possible that Lillian left Mamaroneck of her own accord. She may have been furious that Nathan, despite being a respected businessman, had failed to keep a roof over their heads. Nathan probably could not bear to see the fear on Tom's face or answer the question, "Where are we going to live now?" Lillian's heart no doubt dropped when even her optimistic daughter, Sug, found nothing to sing about.

Once in New Haven, Sug and Tom were split up among relatives, and as might be predicted, this unsettling move, following the loss of the only home he had ever known, would be one of the transformative experiences of my father's life. He was ten years old.

Later in life, Lillian, when asked about how her family's dire situation played out, boasted, "I always kept my head up high." However, according to my mother, Lillian's bitter, absolute silence and smoldering anger at the time of the foreclosure and bankruptcy deeply affected my father, and he absorbed every ounce of his mother's pain. Lillian was devastated by the loss of her grand home on Grand Street. She was heartbroken when they had to sell their treasured Hudson motor coach, and then had to pawn a lot of their personal possessions. She could handle giving away the material things, but she suspected the worst was yet to come. She feared she would pay a heavy price—the loss of the privilege to stay at home and raise her children, and perhaps even worse. Ultimately, the catastrophe would result in the breakup of her family. Lillian was not alone.

My father recalled a traumatic incident that took place one ordinary day when his father had hit rock bottom and keeping up appearances was an exercise in futility. My mother told me it happened something like this: My father was about twelve years old and playing in front of the house when a businessman dressed in a suit and tie approached him. The man was friendly and smiling.

"Hello. I know who you are," he said to Tom.

Tom grinned from ear to ear. His father was well known locally and his construction company had a good reputation, so Tom was used to being on the receiving end of compliments and comparisons. He knew what was coming next.

"You look just like your father," the man said.

Tom beamed. "I'm Tom Seely, sir," he said. They shook hands.

"Do you know where your father is? I would like to do some business with him," the man said.

"I can take you to him right now," Tom volunteered.

The man was grateful. Tom felt appreciated. There is no better feeling for a child than being needed and helpful to his parents.

Tom led the man to Nathan's construction site, where his father was lucky to have been hired as a day laborer. As Tom and the businessman approached, Nathan immediately recognized the *businessman* as a debt collector. His face turned beet red with fury and humiliation. Who knows which emotion trumped the other?

"Why did you bring this man 'round here, boy?" Nathan said. The businessman grinned.

Tom was confused and suddenly realized his mistake. He stammered and stuttered. Nathan was furious at him for bringing a debt collector to his workplace, and also angry with the collector for using his son to embarrass him. Nathan lunged toward the man even before he could open his mouth to speak. The debt collector dropped his summons and ran for his life.

For the first time, Nathan, a good parent, became a not-so-good parent. He lashed out at his son. Tom ducked, barely avoiding Nathan's swing and a black eye. Then he ran for his life too. There were two people humiliated that day. Needless to say, the debt collector was spared.

Soon after that searing and indelible incident, Nathan and Tom would lose many precious things as father and son. They would never be able to admit their mistakes, ask for each other's help or forgiveness, or apologize to each other for any misunderstanding. I suspect their inability to get along was due to the fact that they were both sensitive and vulnerable men at a time when those traits seemed neither practical nor wise.

Rising Phoenix

7

WHERE THERE IS A WILL, THERE IS A WAY

A Blueprint for Survival

*"The Chinese use two brush strokes to write the word 'crisis.'
One brush stroke stands for danger; the other for opportunity. In
a crisis, be aware of the danger—but recognize the opportunity."*
—John F. Kennedy [46]

TOM AND SUG SPENT SIXTH grade with Lillian's relatives in New Haven until Nathan scraped up enough money to have the family return to Mamaroneck. It was 1930, and Nathan's periodic day construction work was just barely enough for the family to afford to rent a cramped tenement apartment across town on Willow Avenue. Although they were better off than most families, Lillian pressured Nathan to figure out how to get them into a home they could own again.

I suspect my grandfather knew he had to design not only a blueprint for a home but also a blueprint to save his marriage. In his eyes, building a new home was a way to restore Lillian's trust and confidence in him as a husband and provider.

Nathan was a strategic thinker, and so I think he conceived the idea of building a skinny house long before the foreclosure of their grand home. What other reason would he have had to hold on to that 12ft x 100ft lot on Grand Street? In my mind's eye, he looked out of the kitchen window of his grand house on Grand Street many a morning, coffee cup in hand, bankruptcy and foreclosure looming, and mentally surveyed that sliver of land between his house and the adjacent property he would later sell to

Mr. Santangelo. After all, he had planned to do well in his business and to build homes, but he had not planned on being unemployed for such a long time. During those months of unemployment, being the detailed and determined man that he was, he began to stockpile salvaged building materials, including planks, railroad ties, abandoned windows, and a worn tub.

Nathan promptly went to work on drafting the blueprint for the Skinny House. The 1931 blueprint that I inherited details alterations to the house and shows front-elevation and east-elevation views of the plans for the second floor and attic. It is dated February 7, 1931, and confirms that the main floor, sides of the house, and large gable façade over the front door were already in place. Nathan signed the blueprint in three places. First to denote himself as builder, second as the designer of alterations, and finally as the acting architect. He framed the rendering with an ornate Roman-style border to showcase his special house of salvaged materials.

When the time came, Nathan had completed a blueprint for a house that would stand the test of time, but his marriage to my grandmother was a different story. I suspect Lillian did not realize her new home would be ten feet wide.

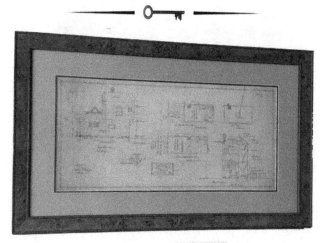

Blueprint of the Skinny House,
drafted by Nathan T. Seely Sr., Feb 7, 1931

8

Our Skinny House

Rock of Gibraltar

If you stop and ask any passerby on Mamaroneck Avenue today, he or she will know of Nathan's Skinny House. Nestled between two large houses on Grand Street in the Washingtonville section of the Village of Mamaroneck, the Skinny House, in contrast to the other houses on the street, sits way back from the curb, hidden from view. *Nestled* is not the best word to use, since this particular house stands alone and casts a shadow on any sunny day. It is a majestic house in its own peculiar way, and quite the complex character in itself. Although only ten feet wide, the house claims its space, and still shouts to all who see it, "I raised a family here! I come from sturdy stock!"

Reusing goods is not a modern-day concept. There was a culture of reuse during the early twentieth century. Think milk bottles as one example. Those were returned, washed, and refilled. Lots of early homes have reused timbers in the basement from earlier houses or outbuildings. Other reused items included shingles, nails, glass, and metal. The Depression only increased the need to save and reuse items that had some value. This mindset—*salvage what you can*—was a lifesaver for Nathan and his family. I think the Skinny House was my grandfather's salvation, because building it was an accomplishment that truly "salvaged" what he thought he had lost during the Great Depression—his pride and ability to take care of his family.

The Skinny House was built east of a prominent stone quarry on Block 64, Section 8, a 12½-foot wide by 100-foot long parcel of the original collection of lots that Willard and Nathan purchased from Marie Denison in 1923. When Nathan began excavating the foundation for the house, he stumbled upon a monstrous boulder of quarry rock. He was a determined man and one not easily discouraged when it came to navigating obstacles in his life. Instead of trying to figure out a way to demolish the boulder, he simply dug the cellar around it, forming a "solid as a rock" foundation.

The boulder in the cellar, which I now like to think of as our family's Rock of Gibraltar, is now dressed in a fresh robe of white paint, and still has not one major chip in it. While it remains the big elephant in the room, neither time nor anyone has dared to mar its dignity.

Nathan built his three-story house upward toward the sky instead of outward toward his neighbors or the street. He undoubtedly realized in 1932 that sometimes when we are handed a short lot in life—literally, in this instance—we have to be satisfied with what we already have, especially in dire circumstances. Given the constraints of space, there was still an opportunity, Nathan figured, to build a house to his exact specifications, and hopefully build one that would please Lillian. After all, designing and thinking outside the box were skills that he owned fair and square, and they were neither liabilities nor subject to debt collection.

The house is 10 feet wide by 39 feet long by 27 feet high and encompasses approximately 550 square feet of living space. A central beam composed of 2-foot by 10-foot railroad ties supports the main floor of the house, essentially double flooring, which is further stabilized by brick piers on a concrete foundation. Nathan shored up each level of the house with 3 x 4-foot studded spruce braces.

The first thing you notice about the house is its asymmetry. Maybe it is the second thing you notice. Quite a standout, the unique architecture of the house camouflages the fact that the Cape Cod and bungalow abodes on either side of it had the same builder. Nathan designed the Skinny House with a grand palette of red wood shingles. There is more than meets the eye. Upon first glance, the house appears to be two storied but is actually a three-storied home. The front façade of the house contributes to this illusion. It is accented with two windowpane doors, two large asymmetrically placed mismatched windows, and three white gables of varying sizes, each stabilized by fancy brackets and trim.

The smallest, slightly hidden gable, just left of the front door, houses a small lattice-like window and one of Nathan's creative inventions—a cabinet mailbox built right into the front façade of the house. The interior door of the cabinet opened into the living room, allowing Lillian to collect the mail from her rocking chair. In spite of the fact that this particular house was built out of necessity in 1932, my grandfather never passed up an opportunity to showcase his ingenuity and fascination with the conveniences of modern living. The largest gable frames the door leading to the cellar, where, beside the Rock of Gibraltar, a black, iron potbellied coal stove, always burning, kept the cellar warm and dry. A medium-sized gable covers the porch, where for decades Lillian's lace or flowered curtains (depending upon the season) graced the front door window. A majestic gable crowns the spindly tower of the house, adding to its storybook appearance. Nathan was determined, perhaps for Lillian's sake, to retain elements of charm and style, so he added a ledge for flowerpots just under the second-floor window and framed the front porch on one side with a white wooden lattice.

The interior design of the house is unorthodox as well. Ceiling heights vary from level to level, and some interior walls, particularly in the living room and third-floor levels, are angled to accommodate the gable rooflines. The ceiling heights vary: 7½ feet for the basement cellar, 8 feet for the first floor, 7½ feet for the second, and 7 feet for the third. This unique floor plan renders the east view of the house its LEGO® toy building blocks-like side profile, where Nathan strategically hung a myriad of windows to create a vista on his world. This ensured optimal sunlight and warmth in each room, so much so that the white walls on any early morning appear freshly washed, starched, and pressed.

While the Skinny House had *good bones* in 1932, it was a *bare bones* house. First, Nathan could not afford to install indoor plumbing, so Lillian and the children had no running water. Water was collected from an outdoor well, boiled, and then used. There was no indoor toilet in the house either, so Nathan was obliged to ask a neighbor whether his family could use her outhouse, located a short distance behind the Skinny House. Fortunately, Mrs. Brooks kindly agreed. Her consent was especially ironic, albeit fortunate, in that for years when Nathan and Lillian had lived in their grand house, Nathan had routinely chastised Mrs. Brooks for using a shortcut through his backyard to get to her own house. Now he had to eat humble pie and ask her permission to go onto her property. Nathan's experience was a good example of the 1932 cliché originally attributed to playwright Wilson Mizner: "Be kind to everyone on the way up; you'll meet the same people on the way down." I am not surprised that cliché arose during the Depression era. It may have been humbling for Nathan to ask this neighbor for a favor, but it was humiliating for Tom to use an outhouse. He was a shy, inhibited adolescent who had only known the convenience of using a private bathroom. Lillian would also become resentful of some of the inconveniences of her new home.

While a lot of the building materials Nathan used in the Skinny House were salvaged, he also desired to use high-quality materials left over from his construction business. For example, on the blueprint for the roof, he planned to use Creo-Dipt shingles, processed with creosote, a wood preservative used to retain oil and color within the wood. This allowed the shingles, according to advertisements, "to grow even more lovely as they weather and to save fuel and tons of coal.[47]" The Creo-Dipt Company was located in upstate New York and magazine advertisements offered customers a list of "reliable carpenters and contractors" in the area who were expert at installing the shingles. Seely Bros., Inc. may have been on this preferred contractor list before the business collapsed. Most certainly, Nathan would have come across the advertisements for these special shingles in a homebuilder's catalog. They were very popular in 1929, and often used in historical buildings such as the George Washington estate in Mt. Vernon, the Governor's Palace at Williamsburg, Virginia, and even at Independence Hall in Philadelphia. Creo-Dipt shingles were also used in Frank Lloyd Wright's famous house called Graycliff.

As Nathan's carpenter apprentice for a while, my father Tom spent many winter afternoons in 1932, his back strained and his fingers numb from the cold, harnessed to the eave's edge of the rooftop, racking shingles and making them watertight. Atop the roof he had a beautiful view, he recalled, one in which the neighboring red rooftops paved the way like stepping-stones to steeples of the village churches.

Firmly anchored to the earth with heavy hooks and steel sway cables, Nathan ensured that the Skinny House could not be accused of partisanship either by the right or by the left. It may have swayed a little in a big storm, as he anticipated and Tom experienced living there, but the house sat squarely as a centrist, and to this day votes to remain an upstanding citizen of the village. Nathan wanted no part of building a house that could be called a fly-by-night structure, and he figured that whatever the size of the house, he would build it so it would command attention and respect...forever.

The 9 x 17-foot living room area is cozy and designed in some aspects like a shotgun house, where you can walk straight through the living room, kitchen, and pantry, and then head out the back door. The family's daybed and Lillian's high-back rocking chair were too large to fit through the front door, so Nathan erected the frame of the living room walls around the heavy furniture. Visitors were always welcomed in the new house, especially if they could play the upright piano shored up in a corner of the living room.

Nathan placed Lillian's rocking chair directly under his "library," a hidden compartment in the ceiling with a drop-down paneled door. There he stored the company work ledgers and the family's book collection. However, my father, Tom, used the *library* for more nonacademic pursuits, such as learning how to smoke a corncob pipe.

Years later, when my father cleared out his family's library for the last time, he saved three books. One book was by the famous Japanese philosopher Yoritomo Tashi, titled *Timidity: How to Overcome It*. Another was the 1931 edition of *Married Love* written by Dr. Marie Carmichael Stopes, and the third book was a 1922 edition of Herman Melville's *Moby Dick*. The triad of books—one on shyness, another with a chapter called "Women's Contrariness," and a third book considered one of the greatest adventures ever told—symbolized to me the complexity of the men who lived in the Skinny House. I will never know which book belonged to which man, but I have my suspicions.

Tom was the only shy person living in the Seely household. Certainly Lillian and Sug needed no instructions on overcoming shyness, and

Nathan would have laughed at the suggestion. Was the book on marriage evidence that Nathan wanted to better understand Lillian's unhappiness and to save his marriage? Lillian was his muse, I surmise. His love for her not only spurred him on to feats of creativity but also left him with a deep sense of inadequacy and vulnerability when he could no longer support her or please her. Perhaps he thought the book would offer him a blueprint on how he could save his marriage with precision and rebuild it little by little, just as he had done with the Skinny House.

Toward the back of the combined living room-dining area, the family ate at a small wooden table with expandable leaves and four chairs. A bookcase with glass doors served as a china closet for Lillian's Carnival glass, figurines, and Depression glassware. Today, many of her crystal pieces that I have are chipped, but they have sentimental value for me and I do not have the heart to put them out in a garage sale.

A linoleum-tiled kitchen and pantry were separated from the dining area by a French-style door with glass panes. For years, Lillian's black cast-iron, coal-burning stove warmed food, boiled water, and baked cakes. At night she banked the stove and positioned the heavy grates slightly ajar to allow a small stream of heat to rise up through the ceiling grates and warm the second-floor rooms. She poked the coals, separated the ashes from the large unused chunks, and placed new pieces of coal on top of the smoldering pile. The ashes collected in a metal pan below the grate and were later discarded in the backyard. Every few weeks, the ash man collected the pile and delivered a new sack of coal. It was not until the 1970s that my grandmother started using an electric plate instead of the coal-burning stove for heating up her food. Where she found a supply of coal in Westchester County in 1970 is still a mystery to me. But I now understand why she never wanted to be away from the Skinny House for long periods of time. She had to tend to her stove. Looking back, it is a miracle that our family did not die from carbon monoxide poisoning or that the Skinny House did not burn to the ground a long time ago.

In the kitchen, a spiral oak staircase leads up to the second floor. Its triangulated steps are so narrow and steep that when you ascend, you have to hold onto the walls and simultaneously look down at your feet, and when you descend, to ensure safe footing, you have to tap your heels back to the baseboards. Today, if the heel scuffmarks on the steps could talk or if the fingerprints on the walls could be analyzed, you would uncover DNA from four generations of the Seely family. Lillian outlived Nathan, and she lived in the Skinny House until she was eighty-eight years old. However, not once did she stumble, fall, or break a hip climbing those steep stairs. I would not be surprised to learn that Nathan had actually measured her feet before he built that custom-made staircase.

The second level of the house accommodates the largest bedroom, 9 x 14½ feet, and a small bathroom. Nathan installed a round, deep porcelain tub that he found in a salvage yard. From 1932 to 1948, until renovations were financed by my father's GI Bill college subsidy, Lillian remained without central heating, running water, or an indoor toilet.

The attic bedroom on the third floor was large enough to accommodate twin beds placed head to head. Decades later, after the house was sold, the new owner, Mrs. Ida Santangelo, decided to insulate the third floor. She discovered the walls were made of "paperboard hammered into scrap wood, an old banister, a piece of flooring and weathered beams of different sizes.[48]"

When Nathan, Lillian, Tom, and Sug moved into their new skinny house in 1932, the company bankruptcy and foreclosure of the grand house were history. Nathan and Lillian were still struggling to make ends meet. They had lost everything, but they were still a grateful American family who had a roof over their heads. The stress, however, had taken a toll on their marriage. It seems to me that Aunt Suge adjusted to the move from the grand home to the Skinny House, but my father never got over it.

Lillian was a complex woman, too, who had more than one side to her character. She was charming and flirtatious on one hand and willful and strong on the other. She had no problem showing her disappointment and resentment when Nathan did not live up to her expectations as a provider. Perhaps in her mind, she had taken a big risk to marry this entrepreneur. Now he was once again a poor unemployed carpenter.

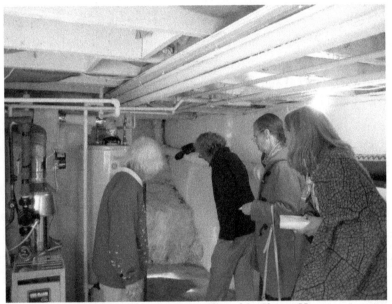

Our Rock of Gibraltar in the cellar of the Skinny House.

Photo taken by Bill Krattinger, New York State Parks,
Recreation and Historic Preservation. 2015

Nathan figured sway cables attached to the side of the house and anchored in the
ground would secure it in high winds and storm conditions.

Despite its narrow walls, the Skinny House accommodated a living room, dining room, library, and family room. Photo taken by Bill Krattinger, New York State Parks, Recreation and Historic Preservation. 2015

2011 Skinny House Gabled Portrait: Descendants of past and present owners of the Skinny House: My mother Doris, sister Diane, me, Ida Santangelo and Nancy Picarello

Not once did Lillian fall down the steep staircases!

Photo taken by Bill Krattinger, New York State Parks,

Recreation and Historic Preservation. 2015

What About the Children?

9

A Beautiful Aria

The Comfort of Music

In most of the photographs of Aunt Sug, she is smiling. I believe there were several reasons for her innate optimism and resilience. Like her father, Nathan, she was outgoing and inherited his confidence and resourcefulness. She felt no shame in having survived a national crisis. For her, the Skinny House was her father's masterpiece, and she believed in defending his honor with the declaration, "Daddy did the best he could." I remember hearing her prideful refrain over and over again during my childhood. She was a devoted daughter, and unlike Tom and Lillian, she never lost faith in her father's ability to support the family or resented him when he was unable to deliver on his promises.

Aunt Sug at a recital. Accompanist is unidentified. Undated photo.

Aunt Sug looks like the model in this 1938 mocked-up calendar.

As a natural performer, Sug was also competitive like Nathan. On one occasion, she entered a local dance contest and persuaded Tom to be her partner and perform the popular *snake hips* dance on stage. While growing up, I do not recall my father ever dancing on stage, but he did it for his sister in 1937. She was one of the few people who could convince him to do something he was scared to do.

Sug was sixteen years old when the family moved into the Skinny House. While growing up, she developed a passion for two activities:

sewing and singing. Even in high school she considered herself more than just a seamstress. She took sewing to another level by designing clothes and handbags that reflected her personal style. Her craftsmanship was meticulous. Every dress she made was lined, with finished seams.

If there was room for a monogram on a garment, my aunt never hesitated to put her personal stamp on it. Her outfits were color coordinated and topped off with jewelry, usually elegant costume jewelry or West Indian-style silver bangles that jingled incessantly and announced her arrival. She dressed fashionably every day. Her personal style signified that she was going to celebrate the day, no matter how boring or predictable it might turn out to be.

Designing her own clothes was an outlet for her creativity. Given the limited career choices for women in the 1930s, creative self-expression was not easy for any woman, especially for an African-American woman.

Though Sug studied commercial secretarial courses at Mamaroneck High School, and spent hours curled up in front of the family's Westinghouse radio practicing her shorthand dictation, her first passion was singing. She had a beautiful soprano voice and her dream was to become an opera star. She was determined to knit hope together and hold on to a thread of a dream, even though it appeared she was all out of yarn.

As a little girl, I admired Aunt Sug. Had she been born in a different time, perhaps her dream would have come true. I imagine she would have eagerly entered a reality talent show today, just for the fun and challenge of it.

Sug studied singing, and eventually opera, during all those difficult years of the 1930s and 1940s. In high school she developed an operatic repertoire that included light arias and classical and semi-classical compositions, but she loved popular music. She grew up in an era when many composers such as George Gershwin sought to have their musical compositions mimic the soulful rhythm and storytelling lyrics of African-

American folk songs of the day. The musical *Porgy and Bess* was such an example.

Sug's shorthand skills allowed her to make a living as a secretary and, I think, as a model. By 1938 she was able to move out of the Skinny House and rent a small apartment a few blocks away on Nostrand Avenue.

By the 1940s, Sug was studying voice with the well-known mezzo-soprano Mme Mildah Polia-Pathé of New York City. Born Maud Pathé in France, Polia-Pathé was the daughter of a wealthy French businessman whose company invented the newsreel and dominated the cinematography equipment and motion picture industries in France during the early 1900s.

Aunt Sug with her famous opera teacher, Mme Polia-Pathé.
Undated photo. Note the famous Bolet portrait.

It is easy to understand why my aunt was attracted to Mme Polia-Pathé as a role model and mentor. Polia-Pathé had a passion for opera and ostensibly led a sophisticated life, having grown up in a wealthy family who lived abroad. I discovered an online auction from 2008 in which a collection of the Pathé family photo albums was sold. The albums included more than a hundred photographs taken sometime between 1910 and the 1920s from around the world, including places like Egypt, Saudi Arabia, France, Monte Carlo, Greece, and Florida.

In 1925, the famous French portrait artist Cyprien Eugène Boulet (1877–1927), whose preferred subject was women, painted a portrait of Polia-Pathé as a young woman. Boulet's elegant portrait is a fitting backdrop for the photograph of Sug and her mentor at the piano. One woman was poor and the other wealthy. Despite their different family backgrounds and continents of origin, they had a lot in common. They were both independent young women who expressed themselves through music and sought to make their mark in the world of opera. The photograph of the two of them was not dated—very unusual for my aunt. In 1958, Polia-Pathé commented on the photograph in a letter to Sug, saying that it was taken during a time of recess just before an approaching storm in her life.

I listened to a 1938 voice and piano recording of Polia-Pathé with composer Joaquín Rodrigo. Her voice was passionate, and I now understand why my aunt held her talent and persona in high esteem.

Mme Polia-Pathé mentored Sug for several years, long after she had retired from teaching opera. The two remained friends and pen pals long after Polia-Pathé returned to France in 1967. She wrote in a letter to Sug in 1986, "I am old, dirty, lonely, aching, and tired." She warned Sug, "Don't do too much for others.[49]"

Later in life, my aunt joined the International Music Lovers Guild and developed a fascination with all things French. She also joined the Committee of French-Speaking Societies, a club on West 57th Street in New York City, where she celebrated Bastille Day and mingled with other like-minded Americans.

At this performance, Aunt Sug got the auto-
graphs of Carl Fischer and his wife.

I would have paid far more than the $1.20 cover charge to be part of the audience for my aunt's first New York City appearance at the 110th Street Community Center on Sunday, July 10, 1949. On that night, she got top billing with Sammy Heyward, the musician known for his collaboration with poet Langston Hughes on the song *Freedom Train*. Her accompanist was Glenn R. Jasper. While these talented musicians have been out of the spotlight for decades, from 1930 to 1980 they were prolific songwriters and musical arrangers.

Sug admired Marian Anderson, the famous contralto and the first African American to perform with the New York Metropolitan Opera. Most Americans remember Anderson's performance at the Lincoln Memorial in 1939. I discovered at least a dozen newspaper articles about the singer that my aunt saved in her scrapbooks, a testament that she was drawn to women who broke barriers.

While Aunt Sug never opened on Broadway, in 1963 she became the star of her first marriage to a musician, Emile Hidalgo, affectionately known as Uncle Michael. Although the two both had day jobs—he waiting tables and she doing executive secretarial work—they managed to travel the world.

Aunt Sug and her husband settled in upstate New York, where she worked as executive assistant to the headmaster of the exclusive Trinity-Pawling School. The couple soon built a custom home in Pawling and shortly thereafter the local newspaper covered their housewarming party.

The newspaper described Aunt Sug as a "Negress." The title "Mrs. Hidalgo" would have sufficed instead of the offensive term. Ironically, the article began with "Love thy neighbor" and went on to describe the warm welcome Aunt Sug and Uncle Michael received from their neighbors, the Hardesty family, and seventy other guests.[50] Aunt Sug was a "people person," and she made friends wherever she lived, bucking the racial barriers. She was the bigger person in any denigrating situation that crossed her path. To her, people were people.

It seemed Sug's philosophy was to "go with the flow." My father might have labeled her optimism as denial, but I believe my aunt survived the trauma of growing up during the Depression because she had this essential coping skill. She also felt that music—whether it was a beautiful aria, a soulful ballad, or an infectious rhythm—relieved pain, be it physical or emotional. She felt music inspired and motivated people. Today the millennial generation might argue that comfort lies in the message of a rap lyric or a punk rock rhythm. I think Aunt Sug would say every generation creates its own music, and ultimately comfort is comfort.

THE BOY IN THE MIRROR

Keeper of the Shame

IN THE SPRING OF 1932, the Sheldrake River broke its banks and flooded the low-lying Washingtonville section of the Village of Mamaroneck. The local newspaper published a photograph of Tom dressed in knickers, standing on Northrup Avenue and watching an "impromptu gondola" float down the Venice-like street. The photograph projects a flood of sadness for me, as I suspect this was my father's first foray into an uncomfortable spotlight. It was his first year of living in the Skinny House, and he hated it.

He had to make do taking sponge baths using a metal tub in the kitchen because the Skinny House did not have indoor plumbing until 1946. Tom waited until late at night to bathe and even then sometimes his mother embarrassed him by accidently walking in on him.

Nathan and Lillian welcomed visitors in their new Skinny House. They enjoyed the fellowship of friends and family who experienced similar hardships and sought to drown their sorrows. Often the evening revolved around music. If you could sing, play the piano, or play an instrument, you were welcomed in the Seely household. But Tom remained embarrassed by his family's circumstances. After all, they were still broke, lived in an odd-looking house, and used an outhouse. He realized the ugly truth of the matter: his parents were no longer getting along, and things did not seem to be getting better despite the fact that they had a roof over their heads. The Skinny House was not the miracle he or his father had hoped for.

Tom was right. His parents' financial troubles escalated during the first two years in the house. They were not alone. In 1933, former Seely Bros., Inc. attorney and investor Oscar Leroy Warren embezzled and absconded with $65,000 from estates to which he had been named executor. Warren had spent most of the money on real-estate speculation in Dobbs Ferry. His disappearance, as well as his crimes, made him Westchester County front-page news for months. Before absconding with the money, Warren had spent time in the law library researching the optimal foreign countries with lax extradition laws. He fled to Turkey after having no success borrowing money from prominent political friends. While he was on the lam, he attempted to secretly communicate with his secretary by placing coded messages in a New York newspaper.

Until his arrest, he had been county chairman of the Democratic Party and was considered a respected co-editor of the *Westchester Law Journal*. A January 27, 1933, newspaper article from the *Daily Argus* reported his disappearance and the gravity of his crimes:

"From a preliminary but not exhaustive investigation of the two estates in question," Surrogate George A. Slater said today, "there appear to be no assets whatever in either estate." A trust fund in the Palmer Estate...was now tied up in the liquidation of the First National Bank in Mamaroneck, and that of the Hansen estate, only $6.02 remained from an original estate of $65,000.[51]

The *Herald Statesman*, Yonkers's newspaper, covered the trial for months. Warren pleaded at trial:

"It was never my intention or purpose to evade the law. Like many others, my financial affairs became involved in the Depression, the nature and character of which none of us could have anticipated. The result was that my mind became so disturbed that I could not concentrate on my law work, and my practice became affected so that I was unable to make ends meet."[52]

Warren's attorney added:

"It is easy to condemn a man when you do not know the circumstances which brought about his misfortune. Mr. Warren has told me the tragic story of his financial involvement, which was not, by any manner, his own making. He was just another victim of the relentless Depression which has brought so much tragedy, misery, and financial ruin to so many of our finest and most respected citizens."[53]

Warren was arrested and convicted of perjury and two counts of felony grand larceny in the first degree in June 1934. He was disbarred in 1935, and his name was ordered struck from the roll of attorneys. He served one year in Sing Sing Prison. It was discovered later that his career

*Attorney Oscar LeRoy Warren's crimes were front-page
news for months. The Daily Argus, Jan 27, 1933.*

in embezzlement extended back to 1923, when he misrepresented a
woman's $3,500 mortgage payoff to her debtor, kept the money himself,
and duped both the client and the mortgage holder.

Given Warren's convictions, I wonder whether he was above board in
all of his business dealings with Nathan and Willard. Warren was listed
as a director and an investor in the original 1925 incorporation filing for

Seely Bros, Inc. Had he taken more than his fair share of the profits and left Nathan and Willard and the other investors to shoulder the brunt of the company's financial losses?

I am ambivalent about Warren. He is to be admired for going into business with Nathan and Willard in 1925. A business partnership between black and white men was rare. Yet it is possible he may have contributed to their bankruptcy or made it difficult for the brothers to recover financially. Warren was not an honest man before the Depression; he showed tendencies to deceive and cheat clients. Does a man's character ever change?

Although President Franklin Roosevelt had signed the Social Security Act of 1935 into law, and the Works Progress Administration (WPA) program had created jobs, Nathan had no luck finding work. One in four of Americans were unemployed. The public jobs created, even menial jobs such as cleaning streets and picking up trash, went to white workers. Immigrants were hired before African-American workers.

Cheryl Lynn Greenberg summed up the lay of the land in her book *To Ask for an Equal Chance*:

> The Depression era proved bleak for black workers and their families as they struggled against the dual burdens of racism and economic depression.... More often than not, however, even in the North, employers did not allocate layoffs and cutbacks fairly, and racism continued to affect employment patterns. Being white doubled one's chance of finding work.... The Depression was hardly kinder to the tiny black middle class.[54]

My research confirmed there were Public Works Administration (PWA) projects in Mamaroneck such as the construction of the Post Office building in 1934–35 and the Waterworks Project in 1937–38, but I was unable to confirm whether African-Americans were hired as workers.

The Seely family suffered another personal tragedy. Lillian fell off a ladder while hanging curtains and suffered a miscarriage. The loss of her third child was more than she could bear. Adding insult to injury, months after the miscarriage, the family's financial situation became more desperate. Lillian had no choice but to take a job as a maid. Needless to say, she was humiliated. She considered domestic work beneath her newly earned middle-class status, a status that she and Nathan had worked so hard to attain. She hated leaving her children to go and clean someone else's home. A queen of her castle just does not do that. She was so ashamed of working as a maid that she would sneak out of the house at the crack of dawn to avoid meeting any neighbors as she trekked across town to work for a wealthy Larchmont family. It did not help when, one snowy morning, she slipped on the ice and broke her ankle. The accident intensified her resentment toward Nathan. Unlike her ankle, which mended over time, her marriage would be irrevocably fractured, and her anger would fester like an open wound. Circumstances forced her to work as a maid for the next ten years. Tom, observant and sensitive, internalized his parents' pain and transferred it into long-lasting fear—fear of owning a home only to lose it, fear of having a wife who left her children to work outside of the home, and fear of asking a neighbor for help.

According to my father, Nathan and Lillian's arguments often centered on his unemployment and why, despite his creativity and ingenuity, he could manage only a few day jobs here and there. Lillian felt he should have worked harder to support his family. After all, she had gone to work as a maid. In turn, Nathan complained that Lillian was not supportive enough of his efforts to get back on his feet. Nathan's pride in building the Skinny House had all but evaporated, and he sought some refuge from his pain.

When Prohibition ended in 1933, it meant little to Nathan. Before then, he drank alcohol only on social occasions. By 1935, however, he began to drink more frequently. He was not alone, as thousands of Americans in dire financial straits sought to drown their sorrows in alcohol. Desperation, chronic unemployment, and family strife fueled the perfect storm for the deadly disease of depression. The United States saw its largest increase in suicide rates in 1935, from 18 in 100,000 surging up to 22 in 100,000.[55]

Nathan and Lillian's arguments escalated until the couple spit fire at each other. Lillian, a headstrong woman, never held her tongue. In her eyes, Nathan had lost his rank as a man and the breadwinner. It was a difficult and painful demotion for my entrepreneurial grandfather, and I imagine for my father, Tom, who witnessed his father slowly descend into an abyss of joblessness, idleness, and perceived worthlessness. Tom and Nathan's relationship, troubled from the moment the family lost the custom-built house, darkened. Still, I found touching clues of their love for each other.

When Tom was fifteen years old, three years after moving into the Skinny House, he sketched a self-portrait using a mirror to outline his pensive and solemn reflection. He gave it to his father as a gift. Nathan cherished his son's portrait. He signed the back of it to document that he made a special picture frame for the drawing on September 18, 1935. Did Tom give the portrait to his father to show him that he loved him? I do not know the significance of the September date, but I do know that, by then, Nathan and Lillian were sleeping in separate beds. This must have been difficult to arrange in so small a house.

The failing marriage was not the only source of tension between Nathan and Tom. Tom was coming of age and showed little interest in following his father's footsteps into the construction industry. Nathan, however, as a young entrepreneur of the 1920s, might have envisioned his son as a carpenter's apprentice. The *American Contractor* magazine in 1922 quoted a bulletin by the National Federation of Construction Industries, which described the benefits of apprenticeship in the building trades: "For economic independence, every boy should learn a trade.... With such training, a man could always find work."[56] Woodworking was listed as number three, behind bulldozing and mortar-using trades, on a recommended list of apprenticeships. Nathan did not understand why Tom would not be attracted to carpentry.

By 1937, the sleeping arrangements in the Skinny House were permanent and a reflection of the tense family dynamics. Lillian and Sug slept in a full-size bed on the second level. Nathan and Tom slept in the twin beds placed head to head against the wall in the third-floor bedroom. My father remembers waking up many a morning and feigning sleep as he watched, through half-closed eyes, his father reach up to the mantel over the bed and take a swig of whiskey before putting on his work clothes. No doubt Nathan sought to ease his emotional pain as he became increasingly desperate to keep his family together and to hold on to his dignity as an unemployed carpenter.

What goes through the mind of a man who cannot find work for a month, for six months, or for more than a year? How does he manage to find the motivation to get out of bed? How does he look at his wife and children and somehow reassure them that he can provide for them? I have to remind myself that this was the era when, in a middle-class family, the husband worked and a wife's most important job was to stay home and take care of her family. In Lillian's eyes, Nathan was a failure.

Tom watched his father in silence, for he understood quite well there was nothing he could say or do. He might not have understood what he was feeling, but he knew what he was witnessing. His family was falling apart under the very roof of the tidy, narrow house his father had built for them. The very least he could do to help his father was to pretend it was not happening. "Morning, Dad," he would yawn.

"Morning, son. I'm off to work," Nathan would respond.

Both father and son understood that, given their fragile pride, keeping up appearances and maintaining a sense of normalcy was all they had left.

By the time Nathan descended those narrow stairs into the kitchen, Lillian's disappointment with him jolted him back to reality. He had no job. I imagine he usually found her standing at the kitchen sink wearing her maid's uniform, sipping coffee before heading out for a day's work. Their eyes probably avoided each other as they moved around the tiny kitchen. As Nathan and Lillian raked each other over the coals, their low rumble would simmer until the unbearable scalding exchange traveled up through the vents like smoke and engulfed my father. My theory is that my father never forgave his parents for trying to suffocate him by imposing their grief over the family they broke up. I surmise he never quite comprehended how his parents, who loved him very much, could cause him so much pain.

I tracked down a copy of Tom's 1937 high school yearbook and discovered a picture of him in the school orchestra. He looked so serious and sad, as if he anticipated more heartache ahead. He served as the second violinist. I still have the silver award violin pin he won that semester. Even though the clasp is crooked, its surface is tarnished, and I can barely make out the markings of the violin strings, it remains as precious to me as if I had earned the honor myself. From the rare times he spoke of it, I know what he had endured, and knowing my father, I can imagine how self-conscious he must have felt performing on stage. After all, he wore his vulnerability on his sleeve, in stark contrast to his outgoing sister, Sug, who used performing and her zest for life as a suit of armor.

*My father's sadness is obvious in this 1937 Mamaroneck High School Mahiscan
Yearbook picture. Photographer: Jean Sardou Studio of WARE, New Rochelle, NY.*

Many times Tom came home from school to referee shouting matches
between Nathan and Lillian. In time, he would become the referee by
default, the one who ended up emotionally black and blue, and ultimately
psychologically defeated. I doubt he ever recovered from being placed in
the middle of his parents' fury and witnessing things falling apart. All the
while, he had a sense of dread that his father would soon leave home for
good.

At age seventeen, the same age his father had left home, Tom's
childhood came to an end. His parents separated after twenty-three
years of marriage. Surprisingly, they remained legally married and never
divorced.

Nathan moved out of the Skinny House during Tom's senior year in high school and went to live with his mother in another part of Mamaroneck. Soon after, Lillian severed all ties with the Seely family, and Nathan's involvement in his son's life was forever changed. Nathan did not attend his son's high school graduation, leaving Tom devastated and unforgiving. Sug, while heartbroken, empathized with her father's predicament, and within a few months, she too moved out of the Skinny House, leaving Tom and Lillian alone.

Tom graduated from high school on June 28, 1938, six days after the great Joe Louis knocked out Germany's Max Schmeling in the first round in Yankee Stadium. Even this inspiring national event did not boost his spirits. He was so depressed about his parents' separation that he never bothered to pick up his high school yearbook. I imagine he felt, *what's the point? My father has abandoned us.*

Perhaps Nathan felt abandoned in some way, too. He had been a father very much engaged in his children's lives, and he had always boasted about their accomplishments, especially Sug's singing and Tom's academic excellence. Now he was unwelcome in Lillian's household, repelled and relegated to bystander status.

While the financial circumstances were still the same for the Seely family, now, by default, Tom became the "man of the house" and had to take on more responsibility. First, he would have to figure out how to help support his mother. That was not going to be easy. Second, without much steady family income or his parents' support, his dream of going to college seemed frivolous. He had no time to feel sorry for himself and resolved to help support his mother as well as find extra funds for college.

During Tom's teenage years, his pastime of reading was his lifeline. He read anything he could get his hands on, including the NAACP's *The Crisis* magazine, for which he sold subscriptions. The magazine devoted a large portion of its advertising section to the recruitment of prospective students for historically black colleges and universities (HBCUs). They included, among others: Lincoln University, Howard University, Morehouse College, Morgan State College, Cheyney Training School for Teachers, and North Carolina A&T College. During the 1930s and 1940s, these HBCUs offered the only certain academic opportunities for blacks seeking higher education, and they produced more than 60 percent of African-American leaders in the United States. Those advertisements in *The Crisis* magazine motivated Tom to apply to college and later enticed him to attend Lincoln University in Pennsylvania.

While Nathan and Lillian subscribed to *The Crisis* magazine, the opportunity to participate locally in NAACP activities did not develop until June 1940, when the first local branch meeting was held in Mamaroneck. At the inaugural meeting, according to the magazine, entertainment included vocal selections by Lillian Seely. Roy Wilkins later presented the formal charter to the Mamaroneck NAACP branch in May 1942. Its Youth Council was organized in 1944.

Tom wanted to become a lawyer, but realized he had an obstacle to overcome. He suffered from such acute anxiety attacks that, when he finally got up the courage to participate in the high school debate team, he had to take off his glasses to blur out the audience in order to retain his composure. Only then could he concentrate on winning. It seemed to me that in this situation, Tom used his father's *fake it until you make it* strategy to get through a competitive situation. Tom excelled in debate, and reveled in every opportunity to dismantle his opponent's thesis piece by piece, rearranging it into a rebuttal as if he were writing an equation. He was so good at debating that by the end of an argument, he had convinced his opponent and the audience that two plus two did indeed equal five.

Tom's social circle was limited despite his participation in school activities. He had a small circle of friends—one, to be exact. Emanual

Branch Walker Jr., nicknamed "Cap," was a brawny and outgoing varsity football player. I am not sure if he got his nickname because he always wore a cap or because he was often chosen to be the captain of a team because of his leadership skills. Cap was my father's confidant and one of the few friends Tom brought home to the Skinny House. He helped Tom deal with his family turmoil. Opposites do attract, so it was not surprising to learn that shy Tom struck up a lifelong friendship with a true all-around athlete.

Emanual Branch Walker, Jr., "Cap"   *Nathan Seely*
Photos from The Mamaroneck High School Mahiscan 1938 Yearbook, Photographer: Jean Sardou Studio of WARE, New Rochelle, NY

Cap grew up in a big family, so his household must have been boisterous and loud. He always had a smile and a calm aura about him. His great sense of humor kept Tom laughing, and I think that is what solidified their long-lasting friendship. According to my mother, Cap saw the humor in everyday life no matter how bad the circumstances seemed. The two young men had a great impact on each other.

While walking to school with Cap one morning, Tom looked at the bright blue sky and exclaimed, "This celestial day is in its glory!" Cap agreed, but later admitted he did not know what Tom was talking about half the time, and he had no idea what the word *celestial* meant. Cap was very impressed by Tom's expansive vocabulary and studious nature. He was unaware, however, that Nathan had made vocabulary lessons mandatory for Tom and Sug. Cap thought Tom was just plain smart, and he promised himself that one day he would outwit Tom. He figured he had the best chance of beating him at a game, so he asked Tom to teach him how to play chess. Cap was a fast learner, and with practice and determination, he beat Tom at chess. My father had met his match.

Cap and Tom's mutual admiration was cemented forever here on earth, and I imagine now that their friendship still endures in the celestial skies over the Village of Mamaroneck. If I had the chance, I would thank Cap Walker for being such a kind and dear friend to my father. I am certain that he had his own troubles and was trying to survive like every other child who grew up during the Depression. I am not surprised to learn that Mr. Walker had a long career in the clinical social services field.

By 1938, the year of Tom's high school graduation, things were changing, and world events were brewing that would impact every family in America. On the financial front, economic contraction pushed national unemployment rates toward 20 percent, aggravating the pain of the Great Depression. The minimum hourly wage was twenty-five cents, and a gallon of gas cost almost half that. The average cost to rent a house for the month was $27. After expenses, there wouldn't be much left to sustain a family. In Europe, World War II started in 1939 with the Nazi invasion of Poland. America went into the war in 1941 with the Japanese attack on Pearl Harbor. Credible accounts of the mass murder of Jews made their way to the American government by late 1942.

Though Tom had been an excellent student, he was not encouraged to apply to college. It was an achievement for African-American students to complete high school, much less go to college. The fortunate ones attended a trade school. I imagine Nathan had a similar thought process—his son could do just as well if he attended a trade school instead of going to college. After all, he had started Seely Bros., Inc. without a high school diploma. Nathan still had not grasped the idea that Tom's passion was for building an education, not building houses. I suspect my grandfather was a bit envious of his son's opportunity to pursue an advanced education, an opportunity available to few blacks a generation earlier.

Tom wanted more than anything to learn for the sake of learning. He wanted to debate the issues of the day, to make his living as a lawyer, and to take part in the burgeoning civil rights struggle for equal rights and opportunities. This was the stuff his dreams were made of. Like many young black students of his generation, he was eager to make a difference. Sadly, Nathan and Tom never realized just how similar their aspirations were. While one wanted to build houses and the other wanted to build opportunities, both wanted to lift up, support, and make life better for their race.

I had assumed that my father had gone straight to college after graduating from high school. I did not realize just how broke he was in 1938. He had his heart set on attending Lincoln University, but there was one big problem. In 1939–1940, the cost of room and board for one semester was $135. It might as well have been a million dollars, especially for a young man whose family was fractured and broke.

After graduation from Mamaroneck High School in 1938, Tom had no choice but to work. Fortunately, he was recruited to be the youth director of the Boys Club of New Rochelle. At the time, Sug was the executive secretary for the local chapter of the Urban League. She bragged to a neighbor affiliated with the Boys Club about her brother's academic achievements, his maturity, and how he would be great at the job. Sug acted as her brother's press secretary and agent.

Tom excelled at the Boys Club, organizing after-school activities for the local community, keeping club rosters, and supervising children. The money he earned enabled him to help support his mother and to save for college.

Still one more obstacle stood in the way of his going to college. Although he had been the first African-American member of the National Honor Society at Mamaroneck High, he had not completed the prerequisite math and geometry courses needed for college entrance. This was ironic given that he would later have a career as a mathematics professor. He knew that historically black universities accepted only the brightest and most committed students. He had to find a way to make up for this academic deficit if he had any chance of getting accepted to Lincoln University.

Having little money to attend night school, Tom came up with another strategy. He decided he would learn geometry and math on his own. The answer to his problem was staring him right in the face. For many years, he had subscribed to *Popular Mechanics*, a technology magazine established in 1902 and still published today by the Hearst Corporation. The magazine featured automotive news, science and technology articles, and invention updates, as well as stories of adventure and home improvement do-it-yourself projects. Its tagline remains *Written So You Can Understand It* and its aim was to bring the advances and wonders of technology to everyday folks. Wildly popular, its diverse cover titles in the 1930s and 1940s ranged from "The Boy Mechanic Makes Toys" and "Make Your Snapshots Tell a Story" to "Rose Glasses on Chickens Reduce Fighting."

Tom sent away for a home study course in geometry and math advertised in the magazine, and by the spring of 1940, he had passed the

Popular Mechanics Magazine and an interior advertisement for a home study correspondence course, January 1938 edition, Used by permission of the Hearst Corporation. Cover design by Harry Speers.

college entrance exams. He left Mamaroneck for Lincoln University in 1940, bolstered by some scholarship money and Lillian's meager savings. Meanwhile, Lillian kept her job as a maid, and Nathan found day jobs in carpentry. In his later years, Nathan worked in New Haven at the Stanley Lock Corporation and the Winchester gun factory. Though Nathan did eventually find work and remained in touch with Tom, the damage had been done. Tom never forgave his father for leaving the family at such an important time in his life. As far as I could discover, Nathan could, but did not, contribute to Tom's college tuition. In 1940, my father headed to Lincoln's campus in the beautiful rolling hills of rural Chester County, Pennsylvania, where his life would change for good.

11

THE RABBLE

A College Life

The Lincoln University Delta Rho Forensic Society Debate Team: Standing:
Doggett, Williams, Seely, Okedas. Seated: Richardson and Nichols. Reprinted from
The 1941 Lion Year Book. Publisher: National Academic Publications, Phil. Pa.,
Used by permission of Lincoln University.

LINCOLN UNIVERSITY IS BEAUTIFUL. ITS campus in Chester County,
Pennsylvania, is almost equidistant from Baltimore and Philadelphia and
ideally located for travel up and down the East Coast.

Initially chartered as Ashmun Institute in 1854 and renamed for
President Lincoln in 1866, Lincoln is considered by many to be the first

historically black university in the United States to confer college degrees to male students of African descent. In 1952, the school admitted female students. By 1972, it became a liberal arts university under the auspices of the Commonwealth of Pennsylvania.

The university has a long history of attracting academically gifted African-American male students. The university website states, "During the first hundred years of its existence, Lincoln graduated approximately 20 percent of the Black physicians and more than 10 percent of the Black attorneys in the United States."[57]

The goals of the university were straightforward: "To provide a liberal Christian education for worthy young men of the colored race, in order to fit them for leadership and service...to train the heart and character as well as the mind."[58]

The university's list of distinguished alumni include the first African-American US Supreme Court Justice, Thurgood Marshall; celebrated poet Langston Hughes; the first presidents of Ghana and Nigeria, Kwame Nkrumah and Nnamdi Azikiwe, respectively; and Melvin B. Tolson, poet, educator, and mentor, portrayed in the movie *The Great Debaters*.

Tom loved Lincoln and wasted no time getting involved. He was elected secretary of a class of 125 freshmen and quickly bonded with his studious and ambitious collegiate brothers. The faculty encouraged the students to excel in mathematics, religion, and pre-law. The Nu chapter of the Alpha Phi Alpha fraternity awarded Tom the Theodore Milton Selden Prize for earning the highest scholastic average in his freshman class.

Tom joined the Delta Rho Forensic Society intercollegiate debate team, founded by Selden years earlier. Its mission: "Where there is an issue to be discussed, these gentlemen of verbal combat were expected to efficiently present the pros and cons."[59] The team competed against several schools, including Swarthmore, Penn State, and Princeton.

Earlier in the late 1920s, one Lincoln alumnus made his mark in the history of college debating and contributed to its popularity during my father's time on campus. Thurgood Marshall became a national sensation in 1927 when, in his junior year, he participated in a highly publicized debate against the National Union of Students of England. Although no winner was declared, the topic was "Resolved, That the Attitude of the Anglo-Saxon Race Towards the Colored Races Under Its Control Is Unethical and Prejudicial to Progress." The intercontinental college debate drew more than 3,000 people to the event.[60]

Tom fit in well with the self-proclaimed *rabble* students at Lincoln. The late Dr. Ja A Jahannes, a 1964 Lincoln alumnus and author of *WordSong Poets: A Memoir Anthology,* described Lincoln's *rabble* this way:

The concept of the "rabble" is extraordinarily important in understanding the peculiar culture of Lincoln University. The rabble was public social interaction, often on display before others in the dorms. One person would initiate a kind of verbal debate. Another student or others would pick it up. And the verbal sparring began and continued until someone apparently won the discussion with some powerful closing salvo that he had skillfully, spontaneously and carefully led up to. These verbal interactions might be grounded in street language or the understanding of the highest intellectual concepts in world knowledge. A winner was often greeted with applause or some show of recognition from the onlookers. Since it was extremely important not to lose face in the rabble, the tension could be great. Often how a student fared in a rabble session was the talk of the campus that day, the next day, and even for months and years. Sometimes a student got his nickname from some remark made by an opponent in the rabble that the onlookers thought was exceptionally on point. In the rabble, the old school Lincoln University student tested his verbal skills, his ability to match wits verbally with other students constantly. Being a "king of the rabble" meant a student was verbally quick and correct. The rabble was constant training for debate, forensic argument, language usage, language creation and general psycholinguistic discourse. The rabble culture was a pervasive, entrenched and a meaningful part of life at Lincoln. The skills developed in the rabble carried over into life. Perhaps the rabble is what prepared Langston Hughes (Class of 1929) for his gifts of language expression such as in his *Tales of Jessie B. Simple* (1933). Perhaps the rabble is responsible for Kwame Nkrumah's (Class of 1939) articulation of his vision that allowed him to lead the successful movement for independence of Ghana in 1957, and later the codification of the philosophy of Consciencism under which he wanted to pursue a united Africa. Perhaps the rabble is what prepared Thurgood Marshall (Class of 1930) with the argumentative skills to lead the NAACP Legal Defense Fund to victory against segregation in *Brown vs. The Board of Education*, or enabled him to become Solicitor General of the United States, and eventually Associate Justice of the US Supreme Court. Perhaps, too, it's this milieu of verbal gymnastics of the rabble that the rich tradition of literary excellence sprang forth at Lincoln like truth-filled thunderstorms and ice-cold revelations, volcanic and whispered truths, and pulsating distillations of a world needing defining and refining.[61]

Tom's nickname was "Professor." Tom loved to rabble. He spent many an afternoon debating with his fellow rabble, the social issues of the day, especially the merits of civil rights under constitutional law.

Tom met his best friend and confidant at Lincoln, a senior named Stanley Sargeant. While the two men came from different family backgrounds, Stanley from a large poor West Indian family in New Haven and Tom from a once middle-class family, the two had much in common. Not only did they both excel in the classroom, but they also shared a passion for music. Stanley sang, played the piano, and composed music.

He introduced Tom to his pretty, hazel-eyed, seventeen-year-old sister, Doris, then a high school student in New Haven. Doris, nicknamed Dee, considered the introduction as her brother's endorsement of Tom's integrity and character. Tom made it clear at the beginning of his friendship with Dee what he was looking for in a girlfriend and wife. He wanted a woman who would be content to become a housewife, one who would be happy to raise his children, and one he could depend upon through thick and thin. He felt that when his mother had gone to work outside the home, even though it was necessary, the family had suffered in her absence.

Dee, one of ten children, was eager to leave behind burdensome family responsibilities. Like Tom, she had inherited a great amount of responsibility as a child and spent much of her formative years supporting an overwhelmed parent. In that respect, they had a lot in common. It was not long before they became pen pals. Years later, my mother regretted not saving those dozens of letters because they reflected a loving and vulnerable side of my father's personality.

Doris Meloria Sargeant was born on February 7, 1926. She was outgoing, smart, classy, and always fashionably dressed. According to her yearbook profile, she had aspirations to become a nurse. After high school, she completed one semester of nursing at Stone Academy in West Haven before her mother got sick and she was forced to quit.

Dee and Stanley spent their childhood years in a third-floor walk-up apartment in a six-family tenement building on Scranton Street in New Haven. Their diverse neighborhood, much like Grand Street in Mamaroneck, was home to first-generation immigrants of Italian, Greek, Portuguese, Russian, and West Indian descent. Residents had one thing in common: they were poor, but they did not realize it.

Dee's parents were born on the small British island of Nevis, the birthplace of Alexander Hamilton. Her father, Alexander Sargeant Jr., immigrated to the United States in 1905. I remember him as an unusually quiet and stern grandfather who had a thick West Indian accent. He played the mandolin, told us kids mongoose stories of the island, and fed us apple and mango slices deftly carved with his razor-sharp pocketknife. He was a resourceful man, a jack-of-all-trades. There was not a job my grandfather would not do, from shoemaking and wallpapering to mending clothes and cooking. He worked a myriad of jobs over his lifetime, including waiting tables, cooking in kitchens, and working the factory lines, taking on any job that gave him income to support his expanding family.

For a long time, Dee's father worked as a chef at the private Race Brook Country Club in the suburb of Orange, Connecticut. He earned a decent salary that afforded him the wherewithal to sock away coins in large glass jars. After he lost $1,500 during the Depression, he never deposited money in a bank again. Instead he opted to invest in war bonds and stash his earnings in a savings account at the post office. By 1932, he had saved enough money to secure a mortgage on a $6,000 two-family house near Yale University on Edgewood Avenue, the bottom floor of which he rented out to tenants.

Working at the country club afforded Grandpa Sargeant a few other benefits besides tip money. He was able to bring home leftover food to his ten children, and he continued the practice when he went to work as a waiter for a dining hall at Yale University. My mother had fond memories as a seven-year-old of being pulled by her two older brothers on winter evenings in a little red wagon to meet her father at the back door of a frat house. My grandfather would place several large, warm tin soup cans filled with food in between her shivering legs to steady the wagon as her brothers pulled the heavy, lopsided load back home. Whatever the Yale students ate that week, whether it was mashed potatoes, green beans, rice, or even mishmash, the Sargeant family ate the leftovers.

When Dee was six years old, her fourteen-year-old sister, Irene, died suddenly of pneumonia, sending Dee's mother into an abyss of grief. My grandmother somehow recovered from her eldest daughter's death;

however, in 1938 another family crisis forced her to leave her family for six months to care for an ailing sister in New Jersey. My grandfather was left alone to care for ten children.

At the time, Grandpa Sargeant worked at the High Standard manufacturing plant, where he often returned home after a shift complaining of steel splinters embedded in his fingertips. On those late nights, in his wife's absence, he woke Dee up to help him remove the splinters from his hands.

While her mother was away, Dee packed lunches for her siblings, chaperoned them to school each morning, then headed to class. It was no surprise that, given her chores and responsibilities at home, she was always late for class, even though Dwight Elementary School was directly across the street from her house. She returned each afternoon to cook and clean the house.

She never complained about taking care of her younger brothers and sisters while her mother was away, and it was a long time before she told me why. One incident scared her to death. It happened one afternoon when her father noticed a white man standing in front of a house across the street from their home. The man stood there quite a while, not doing anything particularly suspicious, but he seemed to be observing the comings and goings in the neighborhood. Dee's father was convinced the man was from the New Haven Child Welfare Department and was ready at a moment's notice to report him for having a brood of children without the supervision of a mother. Dee's father threatened that if she did not keep her younger siblings groomed, fed, and supervised, and the house spotless, they could all be taken away and placed in foster care.

The fear of losing her brothers and sisters at any moment propelled Dee to give up her aspirations to be a nurse and to focus solely on taking care of her family. It seems to me that as a result of this early overwhelming experience, my mother grew up to become a chronic worrier.

In the spring of 1938, Dee's family had a close call that could have easily turned into a tragedy. Ivan, her six-year-old brother, was playing with matches and nearly burned their house down. No one in the family was injured, but the house sustained major fire and smoke damage. Her little brother confessed to the crime only after a fireman on the scene bribed him with ice cream. My uncle Ivan lamented for years that his spanking left a permanent scar on his behind, and from that day forward, he never played with matches. My mother watched him like a hawk for the remainder of his childhood.

My mother Doris "Dee" Meloria Sargeant,
ca age 17 1940

It was a year of highs and lows for Dee's family. Her father lost his job. Her brother Stanley was accepted at Yale on a scholarship. He could not afford to pay the fifty-dollar application fee, so he was forced to decline the admission even though his father had worked in the university system for years. Stanley was devastated and moped around the house for months until a relative offered to give him just enough money to start classes at Lincoln. It was money well spent because Uncle Stanley became a doctor.

Both the Seely family and the Sargeant family suffered from the consequences of world events far beyond their control. When Dee graduated from New Haven High School in 1943, many of the faculty members and about half of the male students in her senior class were drafted into World War II. The senior prom was canceled for the first time in the school's history.

The world had changed.

I discovered a poignant letter in Dee's school yearbook written by faculty adviser Philip Harriman. The letter, addressed to Dee's senior class, was moving because it recounted the heavy burden of war on the young men and women who would become known as the "Greatest Generation."[62] Harriman's letter told America's war story in a few short, heartfelt paragraphs. He wrote:

To the Class of 1943:

I have many loyal friends in the class of 1943, and as this year draws to a close, I wish it were possible for me to send you all off on the road to a successful future with a cheerful "farewell and good luck." But this I cannot do. You are going out into a world so distraught by war that to live a normal life is quite impossible.

Already you have felt the impact of war in many ways. The curriculum has been modified to meet war demands, and it has been necessary to give up several social and athletic events. You have been called upon to buy War Bonds, collect scrap, and to contribute to the Red Cross and the Community War Chest. You have taken it all in stride and as a group have clearly demonstrated that American Youth is always ready and willing to put its shoulder on the wheel in time of crisis.

In addition to this, a great many of you have made contributions outside of school. Some have done volunteer war work, while others have taken their places on the "production front." Over eighty of your classmates have joined the armed forces and even now some of them may be at the "fighting front."

Although war demands all of your energy at present, you must look beyond war into the future. We are going to win the war, and you will be called upon to do your part in building a better world to live in. Do not lose your "self" in an Army of soldiers or war workers. Strive to develop those qualities of character and personality that you admire in our great leaders. Do not neglect the "personal front."

It will take brave soldiers to win the war, but it will take people with courage, vision, and high ideals to make lasting peace.[63]

Cordially yours,

Philip A. Harriman

To me, Dee's experiences during her senior year of high school, as described in Mr. Harriman's letter, were just as heartbreaking as Tom's story of his fractured family and their downfall. Dee witnessed her mother's angst as she sat like a statue and listened to the radio, craning her neck to hear if any of the names of the wounded or dead soldiers were her sons. During her senior year Dee and her girlfriends got up early each morning and went to the train station to see the boys in their class head off to war. She was shocked and confused when she observed the white boys in her class boarding one section of the train while the black boys were steered to a different car at the rear of the train.

The scene in 1943 schooled her to the harsh reality of racism—that the lives of white soldiers were valued more than the lives of black soldiers. It had not occurred to her, having grown up in an ethnically diverse poor neighborhood in New Haven, that her mother's tears of worry would be any different than those of a white mother, especially when the same train might return to the same station months later with rows of empty seats. Should it have mattered which railroad car one's son took to go to war?

After graduating from high school, Dee realized she had missed the inherent signs of racism growing up in New Haven. While she had black and white friends, and had attended integrated schools and movie theaters, she had never had a black schoolteacher. The first black fireman in New Haven, George Sweeny, was not assigned to a fire station until 1957. The fancy department store owners in downtown New Haven had an unwritten but well-known policy of not allowing black people to try on clothes. They were afraid the clothes would be ruined from hair grease.

It was clear the black boys in Dee's high school were going to be assigned to segregated military training bases. According to *The Encyclopedia of Arkansas History and Culture*: "more than eighty percent of black soldiers were trained on southern military bases."[64] The northern black soldiers challenged racial discrimination and legalized segregation. As southern whites became increasingly alarmed by the presence and assertiveness of black soldiers, Jim Crow restrictions were enforced more aggressively, and the tensions between the races increased."[65]

In fact, the United States Armed Services remained segregated until President Truman signed an executive order desegregating military units in 1948. For most of the war, black servicemen were relegated to jobs in transportation, loading, and unloading cargo. As the war raged, several units exhibited courage and patriotism. The more notable units were the Red Ball Express, the Tuskegee Airmen, the 761st Tank Battalion, and the 452nd Anti-Aircraft Artillery Battalion.

In July 1944, the Port Chicago munitions explosion in California revealed the deadly consequences of pervasive racism in the Navy. The tragic event highlighted the hazardous and downright reckless working conditions that black servicemen were forced to endure. More than 320 soldiers were killed and 390 injured when the black servicemen were forced to unload live munitions by hand from trains and reload them onto cargo ships. They had been inadequately trained, and on top of that, they were pressured by white officers to load the cargo vessels as fast as possible.

Despite the disaster, unsafe conditions at the port persisted. Fifty men, known as the Port Chicago 50, were court-martialed and sentenced to lengthy prison terms with hard labor when they disobeyed orders to continue transferring munitions cargo. Their refusal to return to work under unsafe conditions was labeled mutiny. They were, in fact, refusing a suicide mission.

Thurgood Marshall, the Lincoln alumnus and chief counsel for the NAACP, sat in on the trial proceedings and advocated for a formal government investigation into the unsafe working conditions and unfair treatment of black servicemen. In November 1944, Marshall penned an explosive article in *The Crisis* magazine, galvanizing a wave of protest meetings and petitions to decry the unfair prison sentences. Under mounting pressure, the prison sentences for the men were reduced, but it was not until 1946 that the Navy began to formally desegregate its forces. In 1999, President Bill Clinton pardoned one of the last surviving members of the Port Chicago 50.

Although Dee's brother Stanley was drafted during his senior year, at college, he narrowly escaped being sent overseas in 1943. He was ordered off the ship just hours before launch. Dee never knew whether her brother's good fortune was a result of his writing to President Roosevelt, or because Army commanders learned he had been accepted at Howard University Medical School in Washington, DC and judged that he could fulfill a more urgent need for black doctors stateside.

My mother's recollections of Stanley's graduation at Lincoln were vivid. That weekend she attended a graduation luncheon where she collected the autographs of the poet Carl Sandburg, the novelist Richard Wright, and the poet Langston Hughes. Not only did she meet the trio of famous men, but she also enjoyed a rendezvous with Tom before he was shipped off to boot camp.

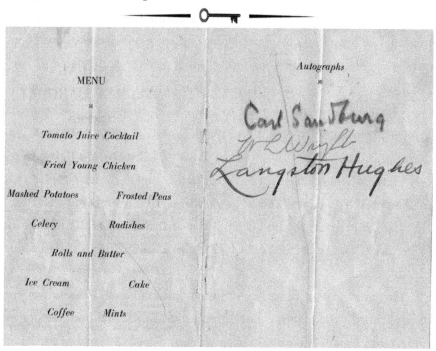

Dee scored autographs of Carl Sandburg, Richard Wright, and Langston Hughes at Lincoln University's Annual Alumni Banquet on May 17, 1943.

Tom was drafted in the summer of 1943, just after he had completed his junior year of college. He was twenty-three years old. I found a letter addressed to him that year from Helen Hird, his former teacher from Mamaroneck. She enclosed an art print he had done many years earlier. It was probably taken from the school's Quill and Scroll Society's *Orange and Black Leaves* literary journal. Hird's last words of the letter were most poignant. She wrote, "In this upset world I hope life is as good for you as possible." The letter was dated February 22, 1943. I wondered about the significance of that date. Why did she choose that particular date to return an art print done by one of her students more than ten years earlier? I did not have to search long. On that date in the national news, three German university students, identified as leaders of the Anti-Nazi Resistance Party named *White Rose*, were executed by guillotine for their crimes of high treason. I believe Tom's teacher feared for all of her former male students, now in their early twenties, who were full of promise and headed to war.

Tom was sent to a segregated boot camp at Fort Monmouth, New Jersey, before deployment to Europe. Even as a staff sergeant in Europe, Tom hated the rules and regulations, the strict discipline, and the required exercise regimen of the Army. Most of all, he hated being considered a second-class soldier and that strangers could tell him what to do, when to do it, and how to get it done. He saw no frontline action. By 1946, supported by the GI Bill, he was fortunate enough to return to Veterans Village dormitory at Lincoln as a senior student—fortunate, but still poor.

My mother allowed me to go through her mementos. I found a scrap of paper torn from a yellow-lined composition pad. She had saved it all these years because it was the remnants of a love letter my father had written to her during his senior year at Lincoln. The two paragraphs that survived were intimate enough to reveal the depth of his love. At the time,

On February 22, 1943, Miss Hird wrote in her letter to Tom:
"Each time I see it I think again how very fine it is, its rhythmic
movement and dark and light quality is excellent."

My father is the soldier standing center. His squadron members are
unidentified. Photo taken by Harry Dutchyshyn, Monmouth, N. J., ca 1943

he had no real prospects for a job and was surviving on the meager $22 in veteran's pay he received every other week. Most of that he turned over to his mother, Lillian. These were not the greatest circumstances for a man who wanted to propose marriage to his girlfriend.

Four short sentences revealed his passion and pathos:

I wanted to write you sooner but I didn't know till today whether I could come up. At the moment, everything and everyone but you seem to be against me. I have very little money and what's more I had to work Saturday. But for the fact that I have you and our love, I would be inconsolably lost and unhappy.

He lamented:

What peace is there for tortured souls? In bondage to the whims of a lady's smile; to the sweetness of a lady's kiss. What peace is there for guileless souls in awe at whispered words from crimson lips, at dainty sighs on fragrant breath?
I really must love you. I never thought I had any poetry in me until I started to think about you.

After reading the letter, I wanted to know whom my father thought was against him and why he had felt so alone. My mother cleared up the mystery.

Tom was a private person, and he had not told Lillian or Sug that he had a serious girlfriend, much less that he intended to propose to her. When he did finally reveal his plans to marry, both his mother and sister objected vehemently. They tried to talk him out of marrying anyone—especially a poor girl from New Haven whom Sug felt was not worldly enough for her brother. Lillian and Sug had high expectations for Tom, and in their minds, no woman was good enough for the star of the Seely family.

There were other reasons Lillian and Sug did not want Tom to marry. At the time, Lillian was living on her Social Security income and was also dependent on the money Tom regularly sent. While Tom was serving in the Army from 1943 to 1946, he sent his entire paycheck to his mother in Mamaroneck. After all, the Army supplied him room and board. It was no hardship for him to send the money. If they hadn't needed it, he could have used the money for other things or banked it for his future. He realized his GI paycheck helped his mother renovate the Skinny House with toilets and indoor plumbing. If Tom married Dee, Lillian surmised correctly, his financial priorities and personal commitments would shift from supporting her to providing for his new wife.

According to my mother, there was another reason Lillian disapproved of Tom's plans to marry. The original house Nathan had built for her, the one he had lost to foreclosure, was listed for sale. There was an opportunity, Lillian thought, for Tom to buy the house back for her. In fact, she and Sug were counting on him to buy the large house back so Lillian could move out of the Skinny House. This was never to happen. I can imagine my grandmother's disappointment, as well as my father's guilt and torment in trying to decide what to do. Should he remain loyal to his mother or should he become a loyal husband to his fiancée? It remains an age-old dilemma for any son, in any family, in any part of the world.

In the end, my father chose to commit to the new woman in his life, my mother, Dee Sargeant, the sister of his college buddy and the woman who would bear him five children.

When Tom returned to college after the war, he excelled academically. He graduated cum laude and earned the honor of giving the salutatory graduation speech in 1947. I would love to have been there, not only to hear his speech but also to hear the guest speakers. Delivering speeches that day were Ralph J. Bunche, the celebrated diplomat and first African American to win the Nobel Peace Prize, and Lincoln alumnus Thurgood Marshall.

Student enrollment swelled at Lincoln after the war when servicemen returned to complete their degrees thanks to the GI Bill. The college was desperate for math and science professors. In May 1947, Tom was offered a position in the math department. Although the job was not one he sought, calculations and equations came easy to him, and he valued the perks of the position, including free health care and housing for newlyweds.

Tom and Dee married at St. Luke's Episcopal Church in New Haven on July 17, 1947. Grandpa Sargeant had scraped up enough money to pay for a big wedding because he felt Dee had given up so much of her childhood to take care of her siblings and she deserved a special celebration.

My parents. St Lukes Episcopal Church,
New Haven Ct., July 1947.

Despite their reservations, Lillian and Sug came to the wedding. Nathan did not attend, even though he lived around the corner from the church. He gave the newlyweds $40 and his blessing. My mother liked Nathan because he was always kind to her.

That fall, Tom began teaching, and Dee took a job on campus as a telephone switchboard operator. They lived in a tiny barracks-style house on Lincoln's campus in Veterans' Village, a section reserved for married students. Tom furnished their new home with furniture he bought on credit. For the first time in his life, my father was truly happy. He beamed whenever his students called him "Prof. Seely."

The newlyweds mingled with families whose top priority was getting a college education and serving their communities. Professor Horace Mann Bond, the first African-American president of Lincoln University, had taken office in 1945 and under his leadership the university thrived and expanded, not only in funding but also in capital expenditures for classrooms and dormitories. Many years later, whenever my mother saw Professor Bond's son, Julian, on television, she could not believe the seven-year-old boy knocking on her door for trick or treat in 1948 had grown up to become a prominent modern-day civil rights activist.

Tom and Dee spent evenings in their tiny living room, twirling around their new record player in their make-believe ballroom. They learned how to square dance under the roof of the university's barn. It was difficult for Dee to make friends because most of the Army wives were much older than she, at least from her twenty-one-year-old perspective. She was surprised, but happy, when the faculty wives invited her to join their monthly book club discussions.

The first book they read, *Sexual Behavior in the Human Male* by Dr. Alfred Kinsey, was just hot off the press in January 1948. The book, while considered groundbreaking in the field of human psychology, was considered risqué in conservative circles. As the newlywed member of the group, Dee was unanimously elected by the older members to check out the book from the campus library. They convinced her to sign it out under Tom's name instead of her own. Given Lincoln's small campus, they may have been too afraid their professor husbands would discover their curiosity about sex. They couldn't wait to hear my mother's opinion about the book. My naïve mother never realized why she had been aggressively recruited to join the book club. I laughed when I heard the story and did not have the heart to tell her my thoughts on why she was chosen to be the library checkout girl for the women's group. Apparently, Dee learned something from Kinsey's book, because six months later she was pregnant with her first-born children, fraternal twins, my brother Nate and sister Diane.

Dee Sargeant, now Mrs. Tom Seely. Taken
on Lincoln's campus, ca. 1947-1948

Until the summer after their marriage, Tom had never taken Dee to Mamaroneck to see the Skinny House. He was too ashamed. She had gotten close to seeing the house a few times. Once they took the train to Mamaroneck to spend Thanksgiving at Sug's place. As the train rumbled past New York City toward Mamaroneck, Tom grew silent. His face flushed. He took out pen and paper, and with sweaty palms, he sketched the Skinny House for Dee. He felt he had to explain to her why he was so ashamed of the place where his secret life began and his father's legacy remained. He wanted to prepare her for the shock of seeing the house. However, the more Dee asked questions, the more Tom sweated and mopped his forehead with his handkerchief. She decided it was best for her to stop asking questions and simply to listen to his story.

In Tom's eyes, the Skinny House was a monstrosity because it was built right next door to the grand house they had lived in. It served as a daily reminder of the family's emotional trauma and all the precious things they had lost. After Tom shared his story, Dee told him that the size of the house he had grown up in made no difference to her. She reassured him that she would keep her end of the bargain in their new marriage by making their family her priority, and she would not work outside the home. After all, she knew firsthand how her mother's temporary absences had disrupted her childhood. Dee finally realized the emotional significance of the Skinny House in Tom's life.

When they arrived in Mamaroneck, Tom was still not convinced Dee would not laugh at the Skinny House, so he figured out a way to confine her to Sug's apartment on Nostrand Avenue for the duration of their visit. He would take her to visit the house another time, he promised.

He made a second halfhearted attempt to show the house to Dee on another occasion. This time he drove her along Grand Street so fast that she saw nothing but a blur. She pretended she had seen the house just to make him feel at ease.

Tom finally got up the courage to take Dee home to Mamaroneck a year after they were married. She got out of their old Chevy, and for the first time, she faced the Skinny House. She smiled. For a woman who had grown up in a household of ten children, at times with two babies sharing a crib and a tribe of children in one bedroom, the Skinny House looked compact, tidy, and practical to her. *What is he talking about? This is a house.... It is small, yes, but it is a house.* She could hear her father's favorite refrain—*Whatever you have is good enough as long as you have a roof over your head.*

Tom gave Dee a tour of the house and showed her how to navigate the steep stairs in the kitchen without falling. It was the first time in a long time that my father's angst evaporated.

12

A Separate Life

Southern Living

In 1949, Nate and Diane were born in a small rural hospital in West Grove, a few short miles from Lincoln's campus. The "hospital" was actually a converted three-story clapboard house. Dee was relegated to the attic level during her labor, where it was easy for the nurses to ignore a patient's request for pain medications.

Diane was the smaller twin, in breech position, and the doctor had to turn her around in the womb before delivering her head with metal forceps.

She survived her traumatic birth, but she struggled to keep up with other children from the moment she was born. The white delivery nurses did a double-take when they saw Dee's newborn twins—one an eight-pound boy, blond with blue eyes, and the other a brown-haired, hazel-eyed girl who weighed only five pounds. The twins even got a picture in the local newspaper.

Tom's life as a family man was the main reason he decided to teach math instead of becoming an attorney. He decided that educating a new generation of students, especially in higher mathematics at HBCUs, would be a fulfilling way to give back to his community, plus the salary was darn good.

To do this, he pursued a graduate degree in mathematics at the University of Pennsylvania. For a full year, three times a week, he boarded a commuter bus to Philadelphia for the one-way, ninety-minute trip to the urban campus. He earned a master's degree in 1949. Dee was so overwhelmed with caring for the babies that she did not get to attend his degree ceremony.

Soon after the twins were born, Tom was faced with a new problem. His teaching post at Lincoln was eliminated after the population of students returned to prewar low levels. He had to find another job, and as soon as possible. Now he had a wife and two babies to support.

Just about this time, many HBCUs in the south were seeking national or regional academic accreditation. To meet the grade, they needed to attract the best and brightest teachers with generous salaries and campus housing. The move to attain higher professional standards prompted university presidents to recruit from a larger pool of trained black teachers in northern locales.

Lured by the $3,500 annual salary, Tom accepted a position in the mathematics department at Arkansas Agricultural, Mechanical & Normal

My father—the soon-to-be professor. The photo is from The Lion yearbook. 1949. Source: Lincoln University of Pennsylvania's Early Records Online

College (AM&N) in Pine Bluff, hundreds of miles away from everyone he and Dee knew. Formerly called the Branch Normal College, the school was created in 1873 to train teachers. In 1892, it was designated as a land grant institution under the second Morrill Act of 1890, passed by the state legislature to educate blacks separately.[66] Later, in 1972, AM&N merged with the University of Arkansas system and became known as the University of Arkansas at Pine Bluff (UAPB).

In the fall of 1949, Tom and Dee packed up their old Buick with precious cargo: six-month-old twins sleeping on a baby carriage mattress, some clothes, and enough canned fuel to heat up baby formula along the way. They started the journey knowing that as blacks traveling through Tennessee, the state where the Ku Klux Klan originated, there would be no motels or hotels to welcome them. Instead, they would have to rely on a spotty network of friends along the way who could let them rest, wash up, and stay overnight.

The police stopped them once looking for a fugitive. Without muttering more than three words, the officer inspected the car and then instructed Tom to "Move on, boy." Later that night, Tom pulled over to the side of a road to take a nap. He awoke to the abrupt sounds of gunfire and the red flash of a shotgun. He sped off and drove the next few hours without saying a word to Dee.

The two northerners were aware that Arkansas had laws that mandated separate educational institutions for blacks. They were also aware that the racist system of Jim Crow outlawed the physical mixing of blacks and whites and mandated segregated public facilities. There was nothing more terrifying to Tom than relocating his family near KKK territory, where mob violence against blacks, especially lynching, was still a real threat. However, he remained loyal to his mission of teaching at such an honorable black institution. He figured that, as a professor, he could provide a safe harbor for Dee and the twins on the secluded college campus located in the beautiful basin of the Arkansas River.

Arkansas had recently garnered the national spotlight. In February 1948, the University of Arkansas School of Law, in spite of much protest, admitted Silas Herbert Hunt, its first black law student. Unfortunately, Hunt's tenure as a law student was cut short. Less than a year later, in April 1949, he died from tuberculosis. More than fifty years later, in 2008, Hunt was awarded a posthumous law degree.[67]

Tom and Dee arrived safely on AM&N's campus not a minute too soon. Their secondhand car, coaxed into staying alive for the last ten miles, finally sputtered, coasted, and died as if it knew its mission was accomplished. The car was at peace. The couple said a prayer, too, for their good fortune. And by this point, even with infant twins, they did not mind living in a dormitory for two weeks until their house on campus was refurbished.

Dee was excited to see her new home. The small faculty cottages, all painted brilliant white, were arranged in a semicircle. Had it not been for the rainbow of shutter colors, she would have been hard-pressed to know the one with the blinking blue shutters was their new home. The faculty houses were located close to the river. Dee looked across the water and saw a poor black neighborhood of randomly placed makeshift shacks. She felt that she was a million miles away, as if she lived on the right side of the tracks, protected by a world of academia and privilege. However, the occasional appearance of a wild hog wandering in their backyard brought her back to reality. They were in the rich agricultural area of the Arkansas Delta, where crops of cotton and soybeans fed by creeks, streams, and bayous stretched for miles. Cattle and poultry farms thrived, timber fell, and catfish was abundant. This was land—earthy, fertile, rich, and ruled by white people.

They had arrived at AM&N at an opportune time. Six years before, Dr. Lawrence A. Davis Sr., at the age of twenty-nine, had been named president of the college. According to a historical overview of the University, at www.uapb.edu, Dr. Davis propelled "unprecedented growth, as new facilities were built to accommodate student, faculty and staff." Years later, his son, Dr. Lawrence A. Davis Jr., became chancellor of the university from 1991 to 2013 and gave the college, then known as the University of Arkansas at Pine Bluff, the moniker "Flagship of the Delta."[68]

With steady income, Tom was able to afford a new car. Even though he knew he would spend ninety percent of his time on campus, he wasted no time in choosing a 1949 Kaiser, a car manufactured by the postwar Kaiser-Frazer Corporation. The Kaiser, a four-door sedan, shared the same body and engine as its counterpart, the Frazer sedan, but it had different exterior and interior trim. Tom was pleased to see his new neighbor and colleague, Mr. Lockman, an instructor at the college who originally hailed from Pittsburgh, had also bought a Frazer sedan. The two men bonded immediately.

Arkansas was Tom and Dee's home for the next four years. Each summer break, they packed up the Kaiser and headed for New Haven to stay with Dee's family. Each September, they returned to their tight-knit campus community where they had made a lot of friends. The transplanted northern professors lived and worked together, their wives mingled in backyards over baskets of wet laundry, and their toddlers rolled around in patches of yellow-green parched grass and occasionally dined on the red clay dirt.

Dee learned to make the sweetest corn bread and to fry catfish to golden perfection. She cooked fresh, colorful vegetables grown by local black farmers. The college administrator gave them a dressed goose every Christmas. The black professors felt privileged. The poor blacks native to the area were often suspicious of these transplanted northerners and for the most part kept their distance, as if to say, *Wait, you'll see. You're not that special here in Arkansas.*

In 1952, Diane, three years old at the time, developed a hernia in her groin that required surgery. At that time in Arkansas, black doctors, while able to attend to black patients in their offices, were not allowed to operate in the local hospitals. Dee had no choice but to take Diane to see a white surgeon. When she arrived at the surgeon's office, the waiting room had a separate small area, practically the size of a closet, for "colored" patients. It was the first time she had sat in a segregated area. The white doctor did a cursory exam of Diane right in the chair, and judging by his curt bedside manner, was reluctant to care for her. The doctor agreed to perform the surgery at the white hospital, and although the surgery was successful, Dee never took Diane back to him again.

By 1953, Tom felt uneasy about letting Dee go off campus to shop. Local Ku Klux Klan terrorist activities were escalating in neighboring counties in response to the brewing debate about school integration and the imminent demise of Jim Crow segregation laws.[69] He had also noticed that Nate, a fair-skinned, blond-haired toddler by then, garnered threatening glances from white shoppers, so he had Dee start ordering baby clothes from the Sears, Roebuck, and Company catalog instead of going into town to shop. He decided he would be the one to go into town each week to pick up groceries.

Finally, Tom made the decision to leave Arkansas and return to New England. The circumstances of my parents' departure centered upon the harrowing experience of their neighbor. One night, Mr. Lockman drove into town to buy groceries. He was stopped at a red light when a white man in a pickup truck rear-ended his Frazer sedan. When the white driver got out of his truck and threatened him, Mr. Lockman, in self-defense, socked him in the face. The white man backed off, but the next night a band of KKK members drove around and terrorized the surrounding campus neighborhoods, hunting for Mr. Lockman and demanding he be arrested. President Davis was alerted to the volatile situation and beefed up security on the campus. Had he not done so, the actions of the KKK's posse might have resulted in deadly consequences.

Later that night, Tom wrote to Dee's father asking him for permission to live with them in New Haven. He knew that he could support Dee and the twins. Mr. Lockman made the decision to leave Arkansas too. The two professors packed up their families in the Kaiser-Frazers and left sweet Pine Bluff behind in a cloud of red dust.

Change was in the air. One year later, in May 1954, Dee's cousin from New Haven, Constance Baker Motley, a young attorney on Thurgood Marshall's staff at the NAACP Legal Defense and Educational Fund, worked on the landmark *Brown v. Board of Education of Topeka*[70] civil rights court case that set in motion the desegregation of public schools. Three years later in 1957, nine black students, called the Little Rock Nine, tested the Supreme Court ruling in the Brown decision when they sought to desegregate Central High School in Little Rock, Arkansas. Despite opposition from Governor Orval Faubus, who ordered all public schools to close for a year, the nine students won their court battle in 1958. The state of Arkansas was forced to desegregate Central High and comply with the 1954 Supreme Court decision regardless of political opposition.[71]

After a short stay in the crowded Sargeant household in New Haven, Tom and Dee decided to return to live in the Skinny House. The twins were four years old. By then, my grandmother Lillian had gotten a job cleaning the staff lounges at Best & Co., an exclusive children's clothing store in the nearby suburb of White Plains. To Dee's delight, Lillian would bring home the store's returned hand-me-down shoes for the toddlers.

One afternoon, while Lillian was at work and Dee was home alone with the kids, Nathan unexpectedly came by the Skinny House to see his two grandchildren for the first time. He had suffered his first stroke and returned to Mamaroneck to live with a cousin. Dee was surprised and happy to see him, and eagerly fed him lunch and supper while he played with the twins. She saw no reason to deny her father-in-law a visit with his grandchildren, or them with him. However, when Lillian returned home from work that evening, she nearly choked when she saw Nathan sitting at her dining room table. She glared at him and snapped, "Well, we're living like human beings now." She was clearly alluding to the fact that, no thanks to Nathan, the Skinny House had been renovated. Then she bounded up those narrow stairs to her bedroom. Nathan remained silent, halfway smiled, and kept on eating.

Dee's face turned beet red because she knew that she was in trouble. Lillian had clearly meant to insult and embarrass Nathan by making the point that she now had a bathtub and indoor plumbing in the Skinny

House. It was a low blow. Lillian's comments revealed her deep resentment toward Nathan. Dee was caught in the middle of a dispute that had started long before she married Tom. After Nathan left, Lillian laid into her and forbade her to let Nathan in again.

Tom ran into Nathan in Mamaroneck shortly after his unwelcomed visit to the Skinny House and ordered him to stay away. Nathan was furious. "I'll see my grandchildren whenever I like. Who are you to tell me what to do? Don't think that because you have all this education you can tell me what to do." Tom was between a rock and a hard place, trapped once more between feuding parents. I imagine his encounter with Nathan reminded him of his childhood and the dread he had felt when he heard the muted sounds of his parents' arguments in the kitchen.

Even now as an adult, I remember the crestfallen look on my own father's face when, in a moment of my teenage angst, I yelled at him, "I hate you!" When such words left my mouth, it was like shooting a gun. The bullet strayed from its intended target, ricocheted off a wall, then hit me in the gut. I wished that I had never pulled the trigger. In that particular circumstance, my father accepted my apology. However, in 1954, Tom ignored the opportunity to apologize to Nathan, and Nathan never apologized to him.

Dee was helpless to intervene between Nathan and Tom and she realized she was in a no-win situation. For a while after Nathan's visit to the Skinny House, Lillian treated Dee coldly, sometimes dropping sly comments under her breath that clearly meant to undermine her trust in Tom. "You'd better keep an eye on your husband," Lillian admonished her. Certainly, in Lillian's mind, men could not be trusted to take care of their families. Lillian's comments were quite unnerving to my mother, so she began to spend most of her free time away from the Skinny House. She sought companionship and support at Tom's cousin's house nearby. The bad feelings associated with the Skinny House were alive, and residual turmoil brewed behind the pretty lace curtains.

Dee was ecstatic when Tom accepted a position in 1954 as chairman of the mathematics department at North Carolina Agricultural and Technical College (A&T), another venerable HBCU located in Greensboro, North Carolina. It was the perfect excuse to leave behind the Skinny House and its eternal fury.

Like many historically black colleges, North Carolina A&T has a distinguished civil rights history. In 1960, a brave band of black men from the college called the Greensboro Four staged a sit-in at a downtown Woolworth's lunch counter to protest segregated service. The four freshmen—Joseph McNeil, Franklin McCain, Ezell Blair Jr. (later known as Jibreel Khazan), and David Richmond—sat at the lunch counter daily for almost six months before they succeeded in their struggle to obtain the right of blacks to be served. Four years later, the Civil Rights Act of 1964 would outlaw segregation at public facilities.

The scientist and first black astronaut for NASA, the late Ronald McNair, was another distinguished alumnus of North Carolina A&T. His life was cut short when the *Challenger* space shuttle exploded after launch in 1986.

My parents loved living in Greensboro, and not just because my brother Michael and I were born there in 1956 and 1957. Dee and Tom attended football games. It was at one of those games between the North Carolina A&T Aggies and the Morgan State College Bears that the president of Morgan State recruited my father to teach in Baltimore. My father took up the offer on the spot. Dee agreed with his decision, thinking the move farther north would be at least a first step toward returning to the New England region and getting closer to her family in New Haven.

Before he left North Carolina A&T and headed to Baltimore in 1959, my father was initiated into the Beta Chapter of Pi Mu Epsilon, the national mathematics fraternity, at the University of North Carolina. His exposure and position in the mathematics department afforded him access to information about graduate research fellowship programs. When my mother realized that my father had never considered applying for any fellowships for himself, she was livid. She could not understand why he would pass up an opportunity for further academic achievement if he knew he was qualified. My father made every excuse for not applying, but my mother never let up. He finally gave in and applied for a National Science Foundation Faculty Fellowship in mathematics at the Courant Institute of Mathematical Sciences at New York University (NYU). He began the NYU program in June 1959. He accepted a teaching position at Morgan State at the same time and convinced Morgan's administrator to allow him to take a sabbatical and stay in New York to begin the fellowship. I doubt he liked the idea of returning to Mamaroneck and living in the Skinny House again, especially now with a wife and kids. But he did it in order to commute to NYU. I was three years old at the time. Our stay in the Skinny House did not last long, and after that summer, Dad rented a house for us in a suburb of Mt. Vernon.

My father managed to complete all of his "pre-doc" course work and, as was customary, his graduate adviser assigned him a mathematical problem to solve. Many years later, my brother Nate, a physicist who trained at Stanford, explained that Dad's PhD studies involved a branch of mathematics called topology, an esoteric realm to most of us, derived from geometry and set theory—the study of a collection of objects. Topology focuses on the "connectedness, continuity, and boundary" of an object, and interest in it accelerated during the 1950s. Imagine crunching numbers and equations that help explain why a Mobius strip, essentially a roll of paper twisted 180 degrees, has only one surface and one edge and remains constant even when it is transformed, for example by stretching and bending.

For many years, my father suspected he had been assigned an unsolvable mathematical problem for his PhD thesis. He wondered

*Aunt Sug, Michael, and me in the living
room of the Skinny House ca. 1960*

whether his adviser had challenged him as a bright young mathematician, or if there had been an element of racism in an academic field where few African-American graduate students in the late 1950s and early 1960s had dared to enter? Was my father simply being stubborn and too proud to return the problem to his adviser? I never discovered the answer to my question. My mother recalled that after working on the mathematical problem for several years, one of our Baltimore neighbors, a professor at Johns Hopkins University at the time, urged my father to return the dissertation problem and request a different one. Dad refused.

By 1961, the birth of my youngest brother, Robbie, and Morgan State's teaching responsibilities took up a lot of my father's time. He sidelined his work on the PhD math dissertation problem and instead returned to teaching full-time at Morgan State.

My mother was disappointed for a couple of reasons when she realized that Dad had no intention of returning to New York or New Haven. First, she was concerned that we would have to attend segregated schools in Baltimore, and that did not sit well with a parent who had been educated in northern integrated schools. Second, my father had turned down a high-paying job offer at the Curtiss-Wright Corporation. The company, derived from Wright Aeronautics in Ohio, an original Wright Brothers Company, had established a solar energy research lab at NYU at the time.

My father wanted to work in pure mathematics and not applied mathematics. He wanted to solve problems simply for the sake of solving them. He was not interested in applying math to statistics, fluid mechanics, engineering, or industry. He knew working for a corporation would be about business and would take up a lot of his time. Without consulting my mother, he turned down the corporate job offer and told Morgan's administrator that he was there to stay.

My father continued to work on his PhD dissertation problem for many years after he left New York. In a valiant effort to solve it, he even taught himself how to translate Russian, French, and German mathematics journals in hopes of gaining some insight and validation that the problem was unsolvable. Throughout my childhood, he spent hours sitting in his easy chair working out long calculations on sheets of yellow, lined legal pads. Years later, in 1970, my father did solve a different mathematical problem that he thought would earn him his PhD. But he was disappointed again when a letter arrived informing him that someone had turned in the mathematical solution a few months earlier. According to my mother, he went into a deep depression and didn't want to be bothered with anyone for weeks.

13

Daddy's Little Dilemma

Growing Up Seely

"Daddy dilemmas" happened early in my life. On the day I was born, August 21, 1956, in Greensboro, North Carolina, my thirty-five-year-old father bought an upright Winter & Co. piano. My mother was speechless. He didn't buy diapers or baby clothes. He bought a piano. Needless to say, I was too young to appreciate his gift. I still have that damn piano. I have remained kind to it, despite its role in stealing the limelight from me from the moment I was born until I graduated from high school.

Thank goodness for our next-door neighbor at the time, Miss Vivian Hayes, a refined lady who never hesitated to give my father a piece of her mind. In her didactic schoolteacher voice, she would scold him: "Now Tom, you know better." However, sensing the futility of engaging a former

Lincoln University debater in an argument, she did not pursue the subject further. She thought it wise to adopt me as her godchild and her "Sweetie Lum." I deserved the best, she declared, since I had the good fortune of being born on her birthday. Vivian bought my first box of diapers and when I was two years old, my first doll, and first red dress. I will be eternally grateful to that wonderful woman because she treated me as her own and never passed up an opportunity to spoil me. My mother was also grateful, as Vivian's attention to me meant she had one less child to worry about. She needed the help, because by November 1957, my brother Michael was born. According to my mother, when Michael was two, I whacked him over the head with a frying pan. The incident may explain why we grew up fighting like cats and dogs or why my brother was so hard headed. By 1962, Dad moved us to Baltimore after he accepted a teaching position at Morgan State College. My second baby brother, Robbie, was born in September 1963. Fortunately, Robbie escaped my attempted assault with a frying pan. I found another way to get my parents' attention. I simply acted like a baby.

My brother Robbie and I vied for Dad's attention. ca 1963

Michael and I, like our older brother Nate, have blue eyes and blond hair. We cannot explain why three out of the five children my parents had were born with these recessive physical traits. My parents never tried to explain it and we never asked. As far as my parents were concerned, we were black kids, and when we moved to Baltimore, we were black kids growing up in a city in the 1960s south of the Mason-Dixon Line. That was tough enough to explain. My brother Nate did not talk about it with us, but Michael and I received a lot of uncomfortable attention from strangers growing up, both black and white. They asked no direct questions of us kids, but the inquisitive and sometimes disapproving stares gave away their curiosity. Are you black or are you white? In Baltimore in the 1960s, you had to be one or the other.

This stream of questioning and unwanted attention I believe contributed to my becoming more self-conscious, like my father. Certainly shyness was in our genes too, and with the exception of my sister, Diane, the rest of the Seely kids never outgrew it. As a little girl, I was always sitting on Diane's lap. I often hid in a closet when company came to visit. I complained when a boy in my kindergarten class stared at me. However, I believe my brother Michael was most affected by his shyness because he wanted to fit in...with anybody.

Michael was a happy child, eager to please, always smiling and giggling. He was musically gifted, too, and he mastered my piano very early. In our household, his music lessons became top priority and Dad insisted we turn off the television whenever Michael had to practice. I remember my father covered the piano keyboard with a long piece of cloth because he wanted my brother to learn each key by touch and not by sight. Michael caught on very quickly and convinced Dad to pay him to learn Chopin and Broadway show tunes. It was not long before my brother caught on that his accomplishments, at least when it came to music, could earn him money. Despite his talent and smile, a deep insecurity was brewing within my shy, vulnerable brother.

Michael and I grew up to be close. He was my partner in crime, and as we got older, he never passed up an opportunity to blackmail me whenever circumstances proved in his favor financially. Aunt Sug saved a letter that Michael wrote to her in 1963. He was seven. He asked her for a dollar, and oh, by the way, did she know that Julie had cheated at playing the Candyland board game? I had a criminal record by the age of nine thanks to my brother. He had quickly mastered the art of extortion too.

By the time I was eight, Michael threatened to tell my parents that I had become a smart-alecky kid who was not afraid of mooning the neighborhood boys. The look on my parents' faces triggered spiteful thoughts of revenge against my brother.

As children growing up in Baltimore, we visited Lillian in the Skinny House during holidays and summer vacations. My father figured he could drive to Mamaroneck to see his mother, then take us up the New England Thruway and visit Mom's family in New Haven.

Although the car trips to Mamaroneck were at least four hours long, the time passed quickly in our crowded Chevrolet sedan. Robbie, still a toddler, had the privilege of bouncing on my mother's lap in the front seat. In those days it was legal to squeeze as many kids as you could in the back seat of a car because there were no seatbelt restraint laws. Since my father was the sole driver, Mom had the responsibility of counting out the change for the highway tolls. We had the sole responsibility of annoying our parents with demands to stop at a gas station long enough for to use the bathroom.

In the back seat, there were four kids packed in between brown bags of homemade bologna sandwiches, cookies, and Kool-Aid in a thermos. Dad never stopped at any restaurant. We couldn't afford it. Within the first half hour of the car ride, Michael had wolfed down his share of food and I would be fiercely guarding my portion. Nate would have his head buried in a book, ignoring us all, while my sister Diane asked repeatedly, "Are we there yet?"

My father had a fixation on paper towels, and whenever we traveled, he kept a big roll of them wedged in between the front seats. With five kids and at least double the number of predictable spills, they certainly came in handy. According to my mother, Dad's obsession with paper towels extended to his habits at home. Every day, his ritual before going to work included folding a square of paper towel into quarters and tucking it into his shirt pocket—just in case. Just in case he got a sweaty face. Just in case his palms became sweaty. Just in case.

The landmarks on the trip to Mamaroneck were memorable: the entrance to the New Jersey Turnpike, the stinky New Jersey oil refineries, and the Empire State Building. We got excited when Dad began to snake his way through the cars lining up at the George Washington Bridge. We could count on his mumbling something about New York City drivers. Only then did we know it would not be long before we would see the New England Thruway sign. Once we reached the Fenimore Road Exit 18A, we knew we were minutes away.

Michael and I skipped along the white stone-lined walkway to the Skinny House. We tried to squash as many sour green grapes as we could as we ran up to the front door. We counted the seconds it took for Lillian to peer from behind her laced curtains and let us in. Even though we were the only company she was expecting, she was still cautious, because she often expected another curiosity seeker or tourist to be knocking on her door.

The back door of Lillian's house ended a stone's throw from the New York State Thruway that was built in 1964. Thankfully, a strategically placed line of trees separated the two. The low hum of the speeding cars, depending upon the time of day, either awoke us or lulled us to sleep. When we played in her front yard, we were aware of the tourists cruising by hoping to catch a glimpse of that skinny house.

In most pictures, my grandmother is fashionably dressed, and that is how I remember her. She loved to wear pretty scarves draped over her shoulders and a string of pearls with complementary earrings. She would always greet us wearing artfully applied makeup, including ruby red lipstick. She was the queen of her home, regardless of whether she lived in a large, spacious custom-built home or in her ten-foot-wide one.

During our visits, she would update us on what was happening in the neighborhood, and then serve us coffee ice cream, her favorite dessert. She had a sweet tooth, and we could always count on cookies or a peppermint candy.

Her favorite expression still makes me laugh. If you asked her how she was doing, she would wiggle her hips a little and promptly say, "If I felt any better, I would have to see a doctor!" We would giggle and wiggle in response. According to Mom, Lillian never saw a doctor because she never thought she needed one.

There was a small ceramic plaque on the wall in Lillian's kitchen, a souvenir that Aunt Sug bought while vacationing in Florida. The inscription includes the first stanza of a popular poem beloved for its simplicity.

Kitchen Prayer of My House[72]
My house is small.
No mansion for a millionaire,
But there is room for love,
And there is room for friends.
That's all I care.

Along with the blueprint of the Skinny House and the *Homes for Colored People* brochure, I consider that kitchen plaque one of my most prized possessions.

Michael, Diane, and me. ca. 1959

I have wonderful memories of visiting Lillian in her skinny house. Those were magical times in my childhood, a time when we kids were gables of sorts, shoring up our family, but unlike the static, unyielding gables shoring up the Skinny House, we would grow up.

In 1961, we settled in Baltimore for good. Dad rented a tiny row house for us on Rosedale Street in the west side of town. It was a crowded house with the twins, Nate and Diane, Michael and me, and our newborn brother, Robbie. Mom had no rest with Michael still at home. I began kindergarten. Nate and Diane entered junior high school.

My father had signed a rental lease before checking out the neighborhood. That section of West Baltimore, nicknamed the Hill because it was not far from a neighborhood called Cherry Hill, at the time had high crime rates, and particularly burglaries. The statistics did not bother Dad. He figured he could outsmart the crooks. Once he devised a plan to detect whether someone had broken into our home while we were away. He developed the ingenious plan to sprinkle flour all over the kitchen floor. If a burglar entered through our kitchen window, he would leave behind a trail of footprints that could be easily traced and identified. I remember asking him why he was doing that. He told me to keep my big mouth shut. He was afraid that our neighbors would hear my loud query through the paper-thin walls. I thought he was crazy, but looking back, his inexpensive do-it-yourself home security system was likely a result of watching too many detective shows.

My mother hated living on Rosedale Street. It was a row house with little privacy. Moreover, the property manager for the housing complex was often locked and loaded. He had a signature style. He wore a black stocking cap on his head and drove a Cadillac convertible with a wolf painted on a side door. I recall one memorable day in 1963. I was about seven years old. My father scolded the property manager for hosting a beer keg party in the parking lot of our complex. A few days later, the manager parked his car in front of our kitchen window, opened his trunk, and meticulously started cleaning his gun. He never glanced in the direction of our house, and he didn't have to. He knew my father was watching and got the message. Needless to say, the property manager was unimpressed with my father's academic achievements or professorial status at Morgan State. My father, however, seemed very impressed with his gun.

That brains vs. brawn incident was the last straw for my mother. That same day, she scoured the newspaper and found a house for rent closer to Morgan State. She figured the location alone would make it a safer neighborhood. "We're getting the hell out of Dodge." She hated that it always seemed to take a crisis to spur Dad into action, particularly when it came to finding a home for us.

While my father was afraid of guns, he was more afraid of people. His biggest fear was being beholden to anyone or asking someone for a favor—be it a landlord, an employer, a neighbor, his father, or even his wife.

One afternoon, Dad did not have a choice. It happened on a winter day when Nate sledded down a snowy embankment behind our house and cut his leg on a piece of broken glass. The laceration was deep and bled profusely. Nate left a bright red trail of blood in the fresh snow as he stumbled into the kitchen where Dad, as usual, was leaning against the wall, supervising Mom making spaghetti. When he saw Nate's bloody leg and open flesh, his jaw dropped. Mom dropped a spatula and froze. Diane announced the obvious, that Nate had cut his leg. Michael's eyes glazed over at the sight of blood.

I observed the scene from the hallway for about ten seconds, then raced upstairs to grab a Kotex sanitary pad. It was not one of those modern pads with adhesive wings, but the old-fashioned kind with long cotton straps that attached to a sanitary belt. I raced back downstairs, out of breath, and held up a starch-white sanitary pad, proudly proclaiming to everyone in the kitchen, "We can use this!" Sanitary pads were Band-Aids to me. I figured we could tie one around Nate's bleeding wound. Why not? Nate glared at me and rolled his eyes, and everyone else laughed. I felt at once proud because I was "thinking outside of the box" but embarrassed because they were laughing at me for the same reason.

That afternoon my father asked our neighbor for a favor. Our Chevy sedan wouldn't start, so he swallowed his pride and asked the property manager to drive him and Nate to the hospital, and he did. I guess that despite their egos and first impressions of each other, both men realized that when push came to shove, family came first.

In 1962, my grandfather Nathan had his last stroke. He was approaching his last days having never met three of his grandbabies, Michael, Robbie, or me. While Aunt Sug saw Nathan regularly, Dad made every excuse under the sun not to visit his father. That particular spring, Nathan was recuperating in a rehabilitation facility in New York. Mom pressured Dad so much that he finally acquiesced to drive us up to New York to see Nathan.

Michael and I dressed up in anticipation, and Nate snapped some pictures of us that Sunday afternoon. We must have been excited. I grinned from ear to ear and practiced my curtsy as if I were going to see royalty. Michael could not stop jumping around from excitement.

But we never made it to New York. Dad backed out of the trip at the very last minute. He simply made up another lame excuse, something about the car not being in good shape for the drive. Mom was livid. He had procrastinated once again and not followed through on a promise. Michael and I were beyond disappointed.

Aunt Sug shared those Sunday afternoon pictures of Michael and me with Nathan at the rehabilitation hospital. She told us he stared at our pictures for a long time. I took comfort in knowing that, although my brother and I were not physically present with Nathan that day, we had made him happy just by being his grandchildren.

Dad's stubbornness and ambivalence toward his father were not news to my mother, but to us kids, it was confusing. Why would he commit to doing something and then back out of it at the last minute?

Unfortunately, Nathan died in the fall of 1962. His absence in my life was a profound loss and one I never really appreciated until I became a middle-aged adult. My grief still lingers for a grandfather I never met.

According to my mother, my father did not cry when he learned Nathan had died. He agreed to drive to New York to attend a brief ceremony at the funeral home in New Rochelle. My parents were not gone for long, because immediately after the service my father put the pedal to the metal and sped back home to Baltimore as if he were trying to outpace his own sorrow or guilt. There is no way of knowing now whether Dad grieved for having lost a father he never fully embraced, or perhaps for having a father who never fully embraced him. Years later, he did express regret over the estrangement with Nathan, especially after he discovered several unopened letters from Nathan that Lillian had never passed on to him. My mother never found out what was in those letters, but it was clear my father read them too late for any reconciliation with Nathan.

In 1965, when I was nine years old, we moved to a rented row house in the northeast section of Baltimore City, just off a street named The Alameda, nestled between Cold Spring Lane and Loch Raven Boulevard. Our new neighborhood was ten minutes from the Morgan State campus. Dad viewed homeownership with apprehension, and he vowed never to own a house because he was so afraid of being evicted. No matter how much Mom pleaded to buy a house, he insisted on renting.

Our white landlord was initially skeptical about renting to my parents, not only because we were a black family but also because my parents had too many children. Dad convinced the landlord that, given Morgan State's salary, he would be able to pay his rent on time. My father's financial argument worked.

Our new neighborhood was predominantly white. It was made up of mostly row houses built in the 1940s. Each home had three bedrooms, one bathroom, and a finished basement. We were lucky to have a long, narrow backyard lined with a white picket fence facing a common alleyway where we could play and hang out all day long. Mom hated living in another small row house, but Dad was as happy as a clam. Tight spaces never bothered him. I have to admit that I, too, loved growing up in that house.

Winston Avenue was and still is, a pretty, tree-lined, long and winding street with rows of houses divided by manicured green lawns. The street was lined with chalk-stained sidewalks, front porches capped with green metal awnings, and blushes of brilliant azalea bushes. The block was curved like an archer's bow. You could see the first and last house on the block in a single glance. There were and still are no private parking spaces on the block. On snowy days, a lawn chair or a milk crate, strategically placed in a shoveled-out curbside space, substituted for a fancy valet. You dared not park in your neighbor's parking space, especially after he had spent an hour shoveling snow to clear his spot. This winter parking ritual, though now considered illegal, remains an unspoken rule in many

Baltimore neighborhoods and is still considered a sign of neighborly respect.

In spring at dawn, mist often collected at the top of Winston Avenue and tumbled down until it settled precisely in the middle of our block. There it stayed until the first front door opened and gave it permission to dissipate into the morning light. This idyllic scene begs the question: This is Baltimore City?

The sweet aroma of honeysuckle bushes, waves of silent fireflies, and the morning hum of cicadas marked the days of our humid summers. The girls in our neighborhood played hopscotch or jacks or jumped rope while the boys kicked a ball around, traded baseball cards, and generally annoyed us girls. We grew up as "alley rats" and played outside from sunup to sundown until Mom called us inside for dinner or until the streetlights blinked on at dusk and claimed the rest of the night.

By adolescence, Michael and I had weekly chores. I sulked in the backyard on many an afternoon, twirling an infinite number of wooden clothespins while hanging a ton of damp clothes on a teetering clothesline that somehow never toppled over. I spent hours in the bathroom pretending to clean the sink and tub while I was really hanging out the window and complaining to my friends about how much I hated to clean the bathroom. Michael had to mop the kitchen floor weekly and always did a bad job. The two of us took turns washing dishes until we got a dishwasher years later.

Our neighborhood was ethnically diverse. We lived next to a Greek family, became best buddies with an Argentinian family, and socialized with an interracial couple. One father worked at the Bethlehem Steel Mill, and another worked as a maître d' at a swank downtown restaurant. We lived next door to a man who was a butler for a wealthy family in Roland Park. The kids who lived on this block grew up to be lawyers, social workers, teachers, musicians, and PhDs.

The neighborhood was not without racism. The Greek family next door never spoke to us and forbade their kids to play with us. They attended church every Sunday to pray for salvation, and then practiced hatred. We just didn't get it and played with the kids anyway.

Once my mother took us to a dentist in our own neighborhood who promptly informed her that he did not take Negro patients. Michael and I stood in his office, not understanding the awkward silence. Dad reported him to the local dental association, although in the 1960s he expected little action to be taken. On the national front, there were a dozen race riots in 1967.

Winston Avenue was a special place. It was the place where I came into adolescence and became a teenager. It was only then I realized my sister had a learning disability. I must have been a slow learner too, because I considered her "normal" for most of my teenage years. Sure, I noticed she had such poor coordination that she never mastered riding a two-wheeled bike, skipping, or jumping rope. According to my mother, as a toddler, Diane spoke her first words earlier than Nate. She was the outgoing twin who had no fear of strangers and always had her arms open for a hug.

I saw Diane do most everything normal people do. At our dinner table she was not hesitant to share her opinions on current events, politics, and the Vietnam War, so it took me a long time to grasp that she would need a helping hand for the rest of her life.

As a teenager, Diane read voraciously, mainly pop star magazines. She was responsible for my adolescent obsession with the Beatles because she played those records over and over in our small bedroom. I had made it my life's mission to marry Paul McCartney.

I am grateful for all the years I was oblivious to Diane's disabilities. Her steadfast kindness and family loyalty over the years never wavered and taught me how to appreciate people and things that are different.

Diane never ceased to be my older, wiser sister. When I would lament a breakup with a boyfriend, she would look at me and say, "He is crazy. Why are you putting up with that?" I learned that having good old common sense had nothing to do with whether you are smart enough to solve a quadratic equation.

In 1963, when President John F. Kennedy championed for the mentally disabled to work in government jobs, Mom pressured Dad to ask one of his former colleagues at the Social Security Administration to help Diane apply for a position at their headquarters in Woodlawn, Maryland. She got a job as a file clerk, and for more than ten years I awoke at dawn to the sound of our front door closing when she left to take several buses across town to work. I rolled over in bed, very grateful that I did not have to commit to such a demanding work schedule. The small income Diane earned helped pay our rent and later helped pay for my college bills.

In contrast to Diane's learning disability, Nate was intellectually gifted. Go figure God's plan. By the age of fourteen, he had decided he wanted to go to Massachusetts Institute of Technology (MIT) for college. Baltimore Polytechnic Institute, a prestigious public engineering high school for boys, prepared him for the challenge.

Michael, Robbie, and I walked to Northwood Elementary School. There we learned how to swim at the adjoining recreation center. We begged our parents to let us buy jeans at Epstein's Department Store in the Alameda Shopping Center. Each year, we pooled our meager allowances to buy cheap Christmas gifts for our parents at Woolworth's, where we were able to sit at the lunch counter and slurp milkshakes without harassment.

A few other memories stand out to me. My brother Michael started a newspaper route for the *Afro American* newspaper. Every Halloween, we filled trick-or-treat bags with a ton of candy—because sometimes we knocked on doors twice and were lucky enough to blend in with the next crowd of kids.

We were very fortunate kids and we had a stable, happy childhood growing up on Winston Avenue. I have many memories of my father telling us kids what we could not or should not do. Now I understand, in part, why he was such a cautious parent. Racism was pervasive in Baltimore in the 1960s and perhaps setting boundaries with us was his way to protect us. Looking back, it was a sign of the times.

One daddy-daughter conversation is stained like graffiti on the wall of my consciousness. I was nine years old when I began ballet lessons at the local recreation center attached to my school. It was 1964 and I was the star of the dance class, or so I thought. My teacher, Mrs. Audrey, had high praise for me. Thrilled, I announced to my father that I wanted to be a ballerina. My pronouncement was straightforward. Unfortunately, so was my father's response. He asked me one question: "Have you ever seen a black ballerina?" I was stumped and completely caught off guard. But I got his message: *Get a grip. You are not "most girls," and your dreams should be different because you are black. You have no right to want to become a ballerina. Instead you should aspire to more realistic goals.* My heart fell like a rock.

I did not become a dancer, but if I could whisk my father back today, I would show him how some things have changed. I might take him to an Alvin Ailey dance recital or a performance by the Dance Theatre of Harlem. I would smile at him and expect him to applaud the performance of Misty Copeland of the American Ballet Theatre or of Michaela DePrince of the Dutch National Ballet.

I was an adult before I realized that I could not always count on my parents' encouragement or blessing to pursue my dreams, even though they loved me and had the best intentions. Each of us has an innate ability to paint over our family's graffiti and produce a fresh canvas of dreams. We just need the right tools and the support of a friend, counselor, or confidante. But our dreams are of our own making. My father was a great parent who had his own set of expectations, some quite outdated.

Dad was the smartest man I knew. But brilliance can be dulled by long-ago trauma. Although he did not have a stroke as Nathan did, in some ways he was paralyzed in his personal perspectives. Was it simply because he was a child of the Depression? My father's attitude was not pride. It was much more suffocating than that. He was scared to ask anyone for help because perhaps he would be snubbed. Perhaps that person might think less of him or manipulate him. It was as though the little boy humiliated by the debt collector was a fixture in his mental baggage.

My father's faulty logic willed his glass half empty. Because of it, he never asked for a promotion. He shied away from any opportunities for advancement for fear he would need to get a reference or recommendation and be beholden to someone. Maybe his anxiety would have evaporated if a therapist had pointed out that the word *perhaps* offers several possibilities. "Perhaps" a person asked would decline to help. On the other hand, "perhaps" that person would say yes. "Perhaps" that person admired him and would have been proud to help him, or "perhaps" it would have been no big deal. Second-guessing yourself and expecting perfection is a bitch and will eventually drive you crazy.

Dad's phobias were contagious. We kids caught some of his insecurities. No matter how many A's we got in school, no matter how much of a musical prodigy Michael became, and no matter that Nate graduated from MIT, we were never sure if our accomplishments were enough. My father's disease of self-doubt, fraught with relapses, could have been curable had he gotten psychological counseling. During the 1960s, however, talk therapy was not considered mainstream, so finding a cure for his emotional ailments had the same odds as winning the Powerball lottery today.

A lot of my memories of my father revolve around music. The Winter & Co. piano anchored one wall in our house for decades, and Dad, glued to his piano bench, was the sentry always on duty. Between calculus classes he played for hours, lost in musical stanzas, concertos, and jazz riffs. While I am sure those Broadway tunes were soothing and the Chopin pieces inspirational, playing the piano was a refuge, a lair where my father could "zone out." The piano keys were passive. He had total control and dictated his own tempo. Mom would have preferred that he live in the moment, especially when raising five children. But she never complained. How would it sound complaining about a husband playing such beautiful music all day long?

Besides music, my father exposed us to many different political and religious viewpoints. He was a Democrat, a liberal, and opposed the Vietnam War. When I was twelve, he banned Christmas in our house as a show of opposition to the war. Admirable for sure, except if you were an adolescent kid who did not make the connection. Thank goodness for my maternal grandmother, Dorothy Sargeant. She was visiting from New Haven and helped us run out on Christmas Eve to buy a tree and last-minute presents.

Grandma Dorothy had a quiet and kind demeanor, which had a calming effect on my father. She frequently rescued us from "Daddy dilemmas," which escalated at holiday times or special occasions. At these moments, she acted as a buffer between Dad and her frustrated daughter. While my grandmother respected Dad, she did not get his perspective. Mom opined that if Dad opposed the war so much, he should have deserted his recliner and marched with the antiwar protestors instead of making his kids suffer at Christmas. There was a time and place for everything, she argued.

Dad proudly called himself an "armchair politician." Now I know why. When he was not playing the piano, he claimed a brown, tattered Barcalounger recliner as his throne. Crowned with his spectacles and surrounded by his library of books, he watched a lot of television, ready at a moment's notice to grab a *World Book Encyclopedia* from the shelf and research a foreign country the newscaster had mentioned. I am convinced he would have been addicted to the Internet had he lived long enough.

While he kept up with national news and politics, he confined his rhetoric to our dining room table. On one occasion, I witnessed him leap from his chair like a madman when a politician running for the Maryland state senate came to our door to solicit support. Mom answered the door, but my father jumped out of his chair and shouted, "Get off my porch!" He was not a fan of African-American Republican candidates back then. To him, they were too conservative.

My father was liberal in his political views and in many ways very open-minded. He brought home bean pies and newspapers from Black Muslim street vendors. We attended Sunday school at the Baha'i Temple for a few years, and he even encouraged us to answer the door when the Jehovah's Witnesses evangelists rang our doorbell.

During my childhood in Baltimore, Aunt Sug visited often. I have fond memories of her visits, but had I confessed this to my mother, she would have been secretly disappointed given the great lengths she went to shape my opinion of my aunt. "Oh, she is a little man crazy" or "She is a little flighty," Mom would say. I never quite understood as a teenager what these terms meant. But I knew her descriptions were not complimentary. I thought being crazy in love was a good thing and having the ability to fly away could always come in handy. I kept my fascination with Aunt Sug to myself.

Whenever Aunt Sug visited, she and Dad would serenade us. He accompanied her on the piano, and she sang show tunes and opera loud enough for our entire neighborhood to hear, not a difficult feat given the paper-thin walls separating families. Brother and sister seemed to be happiest when they were making music together. But I believe music served different roles for each of them. For my father, music was introspective; for my aunt, the notes and melody were a wonderful way to reach out and touch someone.

I did not inherit any musical talent despite years of playing the flute in grade school. The musical genes were passed on to my brothers—Nate on the trumpet, Michael on the piano, and Robbie on the bass violin. I mastered a love for all kinds of music. I am easily reduced to tears by the perfect chord, a stealth guitar riff, or a quatrain of moving lyrics. My parents surrounded us with music, and that was a blessing.

In 1967, Aunt Sug came to visit us. My sister Diane and I had to share our bedroom with her. Since we were all women, she did not shoo us out of the room when she had to change clothes. As an eleven-year-old girl, I had never seen such large breasts in one Playtex bra. I fell back on the bed in awe and just stared at them, secretly hoping that one day my breasts would grow into such a showcase. Never happened. It is amazing what I thought about as a little girl.

To me, Aunt Sug was the epitome of a career-focused, free-spirited woman who traveled the world with her exotic husband and sang about love and beautiful things. She never had children. She seemed independent, especially in the early 1970s when the feminist movement was blossoming. In contrast to my mother, who struggled throughout her marriage to find her own voice, Aunt Sug seemed to have it all. But a comparison is unfair. They were two very different women who fell in love with and married two very different men.

In 1972, Dad was forced to consider buying a home after he had an argument with our landlord about raising our rent. The landlord did not want to hear any professorial dissertation on why the current rent was already too high. He simply gave Dad an ultimatum: "If you do not like it, get out of my house and find another place to live." Dad was between a rock and a hard place. He knew my mother would not tolerate living in another rented house. He had no choice but to look for a house to buy.

The prospect of owning a house and having to move was so intimidating to the learned professor that it seemed as if he put on a blindfold and pointed to the first "For Sale" sign on our street and declared, "That's the house." He told my brother Robbie to ride his bike up the street to investigate a *For Sale* sign and to write down the number for the real estate agent...and with that minimal amount of effort and without my mother's input, my father decided to buy us an identical row house on Winston Avenue. Am I surprised he made the decision to buy a house without consulting my mother? No. Unlike his father, Nathan, who I surmise would have taken detailed instructions from Lillian on what she desired in a house before purchasing one, my father's priority was taking the path of least resistance. Surely any wife would understand that.

My mother fumed every time she told the story. Our second row house was not a bad house, but my dad could have easily afforded to move us into a larger, more comfortable place. My mother refused to sign the papers for the new house because of her lack of input in making the decision, but soon realized that, without her co-signature, she would not share in the equity or have financial security as a stay-at-home mother with a handful of dependent children. I think that if she had had the courage to divorce my father then, she would have. She was so mad at him for thinking small. My parents did not speak to each other for a month. My father sat in his lounge chair and sulked. My mother ignored him and watched television. There were no verbal arguments in front of us kids, just deafening silence. My parents' mutual silence and resentment during arguments was not a good example of how to resolve conflicts in a marriage. No wonder I am still working on improving my own skills in that area.

We moved into our second row house on Winston Avenue, which was an exact replica of our rental row house. My brothers were thrilled with the new place because Dad let them choose a pumpkin orange color for their bedroom. My mother just shook her head.

One of the saddest examples of my father disappointing us was when he decided at the last minute not to attend Nate's college graduation from MIT in 1970. How many black students graduated from MIT in 1970? Less than three percent of the graduating 1,500 students were minorities. My brother, instrumental in helping to establish MIT's Black Student Union in 1968 along with fellow students like Shirley A. Jackson PhD, now Chancellor of Rutgers University in New Jersey, was one of many trailblazers for student diversity on New England campuses in the late 1960s. The activism of progressive students like my brother was no doubt spurred by the legacy of civil right leaders of the early 1960s.

I did not understand my father's hesitancy to celebrate his son's accomplishments. To this day I feel there was no justification for Dad's missing Nate's graduation. The details are fuzzy now, but the angst of that weekend in 1970 remains fresh even to me. I was fourteen years old and eager to see this Cambridge place for myself. After hearing of Nate's activism in college, I knew I wanted to go away to a school in New England.

I had made a special dress for his graduation. Diane and I had both gotten our hair done and Michael and Robby donned shirts, ties, and khaki dress pants. The plan was to drive to Mamaroneck, pick up Aunt Sug and Lillian, then head to New Haven and meet up with my grandmother Dorothy and Aunt Enid. We would then take two cars and continue on to Boston.

At the last minute, Dad informed us there was something wrong with the car and we would just have to stay home. Mom suspected foul play and begged him to consider taking a Trailways bus, a horse and buggy, or any other mode of transportation to get us to Nate's graduation. Dad shut down and sat down. We left him alone with his calculus books and *World Book Encyclopedia*. My mother, always resourceful when it came to such Daddy dilemmas, asked her girlfriend, my sixth-grade teacher at the time, Judy Gilchriest, to come to the rescue. Judy borrowed a station wagon from one of her friends and drove us to New Haven and picked up our relatives. With another relative driving a second car, we all headed to New York to pick up Lillian and Aunt Sug. We arrived in Cambridge in time to see Nate graduate. No matter how many times I look at those MIT graduation pictures, I cannot help but feel a little sad for my brother, who had worked so hard in college.

It seems to me my father was repeating the same mistake his father made. Nathan did not attend Dad's high school or college graduations. I suspect my father harbored some resentment of my brother Nate's academic success, akin to Nathan's resentment of Dad's opportunity to get a college education. The repetition of family psychological patterns is striking.

Not only did my father not attend Nate's college graduation from MIT, he also missed his 1975 PhD ceremony at Stanford University. There is no excuse for not celebrating your child's achievements, whether they are six, twenty-one, or fifty-one years old. No matter how many conversations I had with my mother over the years to gain some insight, I still have a hard time understanding my father's decisions.

Many years later, my father regretted not going to my brother's graduations, just as he had regretted not going to see his own father before he died. These one-time events can't be revisited, for "the moving finger writes, and having writ, moves on." This line from an Omar Khayyam quatrain was, ironically, one of my father's favorite sayings. He even paid us to learn the entire poem when we were kids. Unfortunately, he never made the connection. He never realized until much later in life that he was repeating the fractured relationship he had had with his father with his son.

I remember listening to Dad's chauvinistic philosophy during the 1970s when the feminist movement was in full swing. Mom urged him to consider a woman's perspective. Invariably, his reply would always begin, "The problem with you women..." He would follow with a dissertation on what women could, should, or could not do. Mom, Diane, and I responded by rolling our eyes, and my brothers laughed, setting the stage for a family match at dinnertime.

Many evenings my head swung back and forth at the dining room table as if I were seated on the sidelines at Wimbledon. Dad usually won the coin toss and the opening serve. Then Mom volleyed a retort with artful finesse, often forfeiting the match in order to keep peace in the house and to preserve her husband's ego. She held her ground most of the time, but there were many occasions she did not stand a chance with a former Delta Rho Forensic Society debater.

I felt conflicting emotions for my father—love and hate. I realize now that my hatred for him boiled down to typical adolescent protest against his parental rules and regulations, and my budding feminist bent.

The year 1972 was a rough one for my mother. Up until then she had never learned to drive and had never worked outside the house. She had made a few attempts to get a job, once applying to work at the post office. She failed the entrance exam miserably, though, mainly because she was just too anxious to study.

When our neighbor offered her an opportunity to work part time in a small tax preparation office in downtown Baltimore, Mom accepted even before checking with my father. Needless to say, Dad was not thrilled at the idea and conjured up all kinds of excuses to say no. My mother knew all too well that this was a sore subject because Dad had resented Lillian going to work outside of the home while he was growing up in Mamaroneck. In his mind, when a woman went to work, her family fell apart. My mother countered, arguing that a part-time job would mean extra income for the family. The extra money would put more food on the table and could be used to buy a new appliance. My father acquiesced.

As I look back, the new stove Mom bought with her part-time income was more than just an appliance. That ugly almond-green electric range was a symbol of her burgeoning, yet fragile, independence, her newfound pride as a working woman, and her new expertise in tax preparation, one subject Dad knew nothing about.

My mother was a feminist at heart. She had an attitude of *I'm going to find a way to do it anyway.* She let my father win the minor arguments while she won the war. Although she and I had no in-depth conversations on women's liberation issues, she led by example. She fiercely defended the accomplishments of women and held my father accountable for his chauvinistic beliefs. It's no wonder I chose to attend Wellesley College in Massachusetts, where the all-female supportive environment allowed me to focus on academics and have a great social life too.

There were other female role models for tweens like me in the 1970s. Mary Tyler Moore was my heroine, particularly in her television role as Mary Richards, an ambitious television producer in charge of her own destiny on the *Mary Tyler Moore Show*. Another was Gloria Steinem, publisher of the groundbreaking *Ms.* magazine. The list of independent women in the news challenging the stereotypical roles of women during the 1970s is long. Billie Jean King defeated Bobby Riggs in tennis. Shirley Chisholm was the first black woman elected to the US Congress, and first black to run for the Democratic Party's presidential nomination in 1972. A new generation of African American writers and feminists like Toni Morrison, Maya Angelou, Alice Walker, Nikki Giovanni, and Ntozake Shange, to name a few, created empowered female voices in literature and poetry.

Despite my parents' differences on women in the workplace, there was one thing they agreed upon—dinnertime was special. I thought family dinners were a waste of my precious tween time, and I never really missed this family tradition until I became a divorced parent.

My mother cooked most of the time. Dad would grace the kitchen only on special occasions—on holidays or when my mother made lasagna. Baking lasagna was an all-day affair in our home. The greasy, small kitchen fan whirled from sunup to sundown. Mom did most of the chopping, dicing, sautéing, and simmering. Dad did most of the "supervising," but from a safety zone in the corner near the back door, just far enough away that if Mom tried to swat him, she would always miss. I could tell she feigned annoyance but enjoyed his company in the kitchen. She allowed him to be the architect of the pan of lasagna layer by layer, placing the noodles first lengthwise then crisscross until the pan was topped with sauce and mozzarella cheese to the brim.

It is obvious to me now why my father was devastated when his own family dinners faded as his parents' marriage deteriorated in the 1930s. I am grateful for the stable upbringing I had, and I appreciate the countless dinners my parents prepared. However, I wish at the dinner table they had passed on to us kids more wisdom about maintaining self-esteem and self-confidence. We were black kids with blond hair and blue eyes. It would have been helpful if they had open discussions about the scrutiny and disdain we felt from both whites and blacks. We would have realized the need to fortify ourselves with a shield of self-confidence in order to survive not only racism, but also the usual peaks and valleys of adolescence and young adulthood. I survived the journey by piecing together bits of armor over my thin skin. I did it through counseling, by learning to tolerate a certain amount of social awkwardness in new situations, and by finally figuring out it was really none of my business whether someone liked me or did not like me.

My brother Michael never had a chance. He struggled throughout adolescence to fit in with the neighborhood boys and to find camaraderie with them. The black boys gave him a hard time because he had blue eyes and a blond Afro, and the white boys rejected him because he was black. Despite his musical talent, I felt he was never comfortable on stage. Unlike my father who blurred out a debate team audience by removing his eyeglasses, my brother discovered that alcohol melted his shyness and temporarily shielded him from his insecurities. Michael became an alcoholic by age fifteen and swallowed up by depression. Without the benefit of all of the modern antidepressant medications we have today, his disease worsened and his mental health deteriorated. After several stints in rehab and jail, he died from an alcohol-related seizure in 1992 at the age of 35. Michael had latched on to any Tom, Dick, or Harriet who promised him popularity and acceptance. He had never claimed his life as his own. I realize that no amount of family dinners could have saved him from his addictions. Countless times I fantasized about whisking him away to some foreign land where there was no such thing as addiction and depression, where I could control his every action until he could survive on his own and reach sobriety. But Michael's life was not mine to lead. The pain of losing my younger brother who had so much promise still feels quite fresh.

My father was spared Michael's death, but he lived long enough to grieve over his son's illness. Michael died in 1992, three years after my father passed away. My mother endured twin sorrows as a mother and widow would, having lost her talented child and her loving husband in a span of three years. She never got over it.

Legacy

14

FAME OR INFAMY

Celebrity Has Its Cost

Half-House[73]
I am a house, but only half
Such is my claim to fame.
I am a house, a house so rare
There is no two the same.
My seasoned timber never gives.
I'm everlasting true,
What I observe
Through clearest view,
When all is said and done,
The sweet sonnet of my room
Is half of me is better than none.
—Poet Marilyn Ducati, 1973

MARRIED LIFE AND CAREER ESSENTIALLY kept my father and our
family away from Mamaroneck for decades. With the exception of visits
to see Lillian on holidays and during summer vacations, we remained
focused on our own lives south of the Mason-Dixon line. During these
Baltimore years, the skinny house my grandfather built transitioned out
of the shadows on Grand Street and into the national spotlight of fame.
The house developed a captivating personality and came into a legacy of
its own. I would give much of the credit for the publicity surrounding the

Skinny House in our family's absence, especially during the 1980s and after my grandmother's death, to her next-door neighbor, Ida Santangelo, the daughter of Panfilo and Maria Santangelo.

However, people have always been intrigued with the Skinny House. Their curiosity is understandable. The ten-foot-wide house does look, as many have said, like a doll's house. Architects have scoped out the rooms with their tape measures and climbed its narrow spiral staircase. The public has variously dubbed it the "thin house," the "little house," and the "skinny house."

In one photograph in which a black cat crosses its path, the house looks like a fairy-tale cottage. It has generated many local myths. Some folks held on to the story that my grandmother was an opera singer who fled the limelight to live quietly in the suburbs. Well, part of that story is true. An aspiring opera singer lived there. Another story suggested a family of "little people" lived in the house. My grandfather would have objected to that description since he did everything in a big way.

My grandmother is quoted in a 1978 newspaper article as having said, "I've heard a lot about the attention, but it doesn't concern me. I take it with a smile."[74] Her desire for privacy and my father's reluctance to share much about his life contributed to the wild myths surrounding our family and the house.

Once a newspaper made the mistake of publishing a drawing of the house that had not been approved by my grandmother. Aunt Sug quickly responded:

Dear Editor,

I am writing on behalf of the owner of the "celebrated thin house," as referred by Phil Reisman, one of your staff writers, in his article appearing in the Monday, December 4, 1978 issue of your newspaper, on page A3. The purpose of this letter is to focus your attention on Mr. Reisman's article entitled *Tourists*

Add to Thin House Myths with accompanying photo of the house by him. Further, to add insult to injury, the grossly exaggerated and distorted drawing of this so-called "thin house" is very poorly done, and certainly not the least bit complimentary to the designer, builder and owner of the residence.

Neither the writer of the column in question nor the person who tried to draw the house as it actually is had express permission from the owner to take pictures, submit any drawings, or information for the purposes of publication. In my opinion and that of the owner, the writer's story has definitely discredited the craftsmanship of the builder and designer!

I also note that both the dimensions and other information concerning the house were inaccurately stated in your newspaper article. The "myths" circulated by persons of obviously questionable mentality and sense of values are indeed insulting and degrading, particularly your statement: "And there are the crass who sincerely hold the notion that a giant fat man and his wife have stuffed themselves into the house and are living in bliss after selling their life story to the *National Enquirer.*"

Another myth circulating by some inquisitive, shallow observers that "Mrs. Seely is a former opera singer, a great star who fled the limelight to live quietly in the suburbs," is utterly ridiculous! There are also a number of other erroneous statements in Mr. Reisman's story.

My advice to all those who have participated in the very annoying publicity is to refrain from harassing the owner and encroaching upon her civil right to privacy. It has been very unpleasant to her to have people constantly drive by, gape and pause to photograph her house. Continuation of this kind of publicity will surely attract an endless stream of curious people from all over. The owner simply wants to live in peace—which is her right.[75]

L. Hidalgo
Harmony Road
Pawling, New York

My father would not have had the courage to write a letter like that to the newspaper. He remained silent on the matter. Aunt Sug defended Nathan's legacy and protested the invasion of Lillian's privacy. In her eyes, the newspaper made a mockery of the house and by default a mockery of my grandfather.

On January 27, 1986, the historian Grace Huntley Pugh made a plea to the Mamaroneck Village Board of Trustees Landmarks Advisory Committee to designate the Skinny House as a local historic landmark. She responded:

Mr. Seely was a black contractor at a time in history when that itself was uncommon. The preservation of this house would help maintain a part of Mamaroneck's black history. This structure is one of a kind. It is local history and a specific characteristic of the Village of Mamaroneck that could never be replaced if lost to neglect."[76]

On March 6, 1991, the Skinny House achieved Westchester County historic landmark status.

By 2002, the Skinny House had earned a respectable and venerable position in the village. Phil Reisman's article "Skinny House Fat with History" in the *Journal News* summarized my grandfather's achievement and grandmother's lifetime of perseverance:

The "Skinny House" on Grand Street may or may not be a little wider than those other houses (in the *Guinness Book of World Records* or "Ripley's Believe It or Not") but it is . . . a local wonder. And the cause for its creation gives it special meaning. Seely's feat was heroic. Facing bill collectors in the worst of times, he was able to improvise, invent and build with his bare hands a cozy little home for his family. Reflecting on her husband's work, Lillian Seely said in a 1978 interview, "All I know is that this house is a lifesaver after the times we went through." Does that amount to a world record? No, of course not. But you also can't put a price on a man's sacrifice—believe it or not.[775]

For a long time, I did not understand the omission of my grandfather's life story in the countless newspaper articles written over the years about his house. Before 2002, there were no references in the newspaper coverage that Nathan and Willard were successful African American entrepreneurs, and that, against all odds during the 1920s, they owned the land on Grand Street on which three Seely Bros. houses were built. Instead, the articles focused on the odd architecture of the house or the benevolence of the Santangelo family. The house is odd and the Santangelo family were kind neighbors of my grandparents for more than sixty years. Those are the facts. After the sale of the house in 1986, the Santangelo family, as the new owners, became the only local source of information about the house. My family in Baltimore rarely kept up with Mamaroneck news, and even if we had, I doubt my father would have contributed to any stories that focused on his life there.

However, my family's ignorance of what was going on in Mamaroneck was no excuse. I personally regret having not spoken up sooner about my grandfather to tell "the rest of the story," as the famous newscaster Paul Harvey used to say at the end of his show.

<h1 style="text-align:center">15</h1>

<h1 style="text-align:center">Heart for Sale</h1>

A Family's Loss

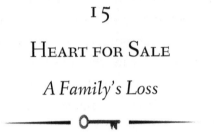

THERE IS A SONG CALLED "The Other Side" sung by El DeBarge and written by Terry Lewis and James Harris III that is hauntingly beautiful. It is about how the very person you love so much and who loves you can cause you so much pain. I connect with that song because it reminds me so much of the relationship between my father and grandfather, and the relationship between my father and the Skinny House. I am convinced the two men loved each other dearly, but they struggled to express their feelings, so they ended up resenting each other. I also believe there was a part of my father that was proud of Nathan's accomplishments, including building the Skinny House. However, the Great Depression made reconciliation impossible because it roared through the country like a freight train and hijacked opportunities for forgiveness between fathers and sons that no amount of ransom would satisfy.

In April 1983, my grandmother Lillian Beatrice Seely was eighty-eight years old and still living alone in the Skinny House. My parents were empty nesters by then, so they were able to make frequent trips from Baltimore to Mamaroneck to check on her. Aunt Sug, still living in Duchess County, also made weekly trips to help Lillian, but it was not enough to ease the family's concern. There were times when Lillian forgot to eat or drink. Over time, she became withdrawn. She kept the lace curtains at the front door, now heavy and gray with dust, tightly closed, not because she wanted privacy, but because she was becoming paranoid.

My grandmother, Lillian Beatrice Seely,
Port Chester Nursing Home, ca. 1982

On the last afternoon my grandmother spent in her Skinny House, dementia, incurable and insolent, stalked her like a vulture. It perched outside her door until it smelled the perfect opportunity to steal her faculties. My parents and Aunt Sug sat around the dining table in the narrow living room and tried to convince her to move into a nursing home. The evidence for their argument was overwhelming. She could no longer think for herself, and she was dehydrated, malnourished, and incompetent to make her own decisions. Her refrigerator was filled with rotting food that the neighbors had so kindly donated. There were large sums of money stuffed under her mattress and between cracks in the walls of her pantry. It was clear my grandmother needed twenty-four-hour supervision.

After a couple of hours of fruitless discussion, my mother got up to stretch her legs and went to the front door to get some fresh air. As she pulled apart the lace curtains and opened the front door, she discovered a piece of pink paper neatly pinned inside the folds of one of the curtains. My grandmother had scrawled just six words on it: "To anyone. I was happy here." Her resolve to die in the house was heartbreaking. She had no intention of leaving her Skinny House. Never-ever.

My grandmother's touching note spoke volumes about her loneliness and about her unapologetic choice to find happiness in the home Nathan had built for her. She had struggled all of her life to move up the economic and social ladders, remain queen of her household, and to secure happiness and success for her family. Now, once again, her fate was in someone else's hands. This time it was her son who had disappointed her because he was unable to care for her. That afternoon she gave my father the cold shoulder. She would not look him in the eye. Dad was devastated and whispered to Mom, "Look. She has turned her back on her own son."

Dad and Aunt Sug told Lillian that they were going to take her for a ride. By the time they got her in the car, she was seriously ill and needed immediate admission to a hospital.

I was scheduled to graduate from medical school in May 1983 when all these events were unfolding. I realized that my grandmother was too sick to attend the graduation in Boston. Although I rationalized the events of her illness like a doctor as an inevitable rite of passage, I was sad knowing that her health was rapidly deteriorating and that she was forced to leave the home she had come to love.

My parents and I went to see visit Lillian at the nursing home. She was still the dignified lady I remembered. She carried her pocketbook wherever she went, adorned herself with pearls, and wore stockings. She fixed her hair every day. It took her a long time to adjust to the nursing home. Of her new home in Port Chester, she would smile and ask us, "How do you like my new place?"

"We like it just fine," we would answer.

I do not think that she ever noticed a picture of the Skinny House on the bulletin board near the nurse's station.

For me, my grandmother's departure from the Skinny House also gave rise to troublesome questions. What would happen to my grandfather's house? Were my father and Aunt Sug going to sell it? It was the only thing we had left of my grandparents. Couldn't we find a way to keep it in the family? I knew how much the house meant to my grandmother.

I wrote Aunt Sug a letter in October 1983 telling her how sad I was that our family might have to sell the Skinny House. Her response was poignant and practical.

She responded:

Yes, Julie, no matter who ultimately owns the little house, it will always be in our hearts as a symbol of Grandpa Seely's ingenuity and hard labor. As I write this, I have tears in my eyes and my heart is breaking. If I only had the money I would never let it go, and would maintain it and care for it as a monument to my dear parents. Julie, we must be realistic, your grandmother's maintenance in the nursing home must be met, and the County of Westchester must be paid. Neither, my brother or I is financially able to assume the responsibility. I do appreciate how you feel more than you'll ever know.[78]

Aunt Sug and Dad decided not to tell my grandmother that her home would be put up for sale or even that the neighbor, Ida Santangelo, was interested in buying it. The idea of selling her "lifesaver" little house and staying on in the nursing home would have devastated her.

I believe my father was ambivalent about selling the house. However, his shame tipped the scales and convinced him to sell it. There are days when I still find it hard to forgive him. Although his decision was quite rational and compassionate as a child providing for his mother, my heart still sinks when I think about it. At the time, my objection to the sale and resentment toward him seemed selfish. It was based on my worship of a grandfather I had never met, but loved nonetheless. I felt helpless. Neither the family nor I could afford to take care of our grandmother or pay her nursing home bills.

One year later, on May 22, 1984, Dad and Aunt Sug sold the Skinny House for $30,000 to Ida Santangelo, the daughter of my parents' longtime neighbors. The money from the sale of the house was turned over to the state for my grandmother's care in the nursing home.

My grandmother, Lillian Beatrice Booth-Seely, died on August 30, 1984. She was ninety-one years old and had lived in her skinny home for more than half a century. She had climbed its steep spiral staircase and banked her coal stove more than a thousand nights. She had opened the front door to welcome her grandchildren more than a hundred times. Her passing was the end of an era for my family.

16

Legacy Matters

Matters of the Heart

Every family inherits a certain amount of "brokenness" in its ancestral lineage, often due to historical events beyond its control or due to personal tragedy or family trauma. African-American families, because of slavery, have a more difficult time tracing their ancestral lines. No matter our cultural background, the quest for one's legacy is so important because it affords us all the opportunity to piece together our unique stories and to make us whole again.

What is legacy, and why is it so important? Webster's dictionary defines the term as "a gift by will, especially of money or other personal property, a bequest or something transmitted by or received from an ancestor or predecessor or from the past."[79] If I measured my legacy by the material possessions I inherited, I would be considered poor. However, I am a very wealthy woman.

In 1985, one year after my grandmother's death, Aunt Sug transformed a basic McCall's pattern into a custom-made wedding gown for me. Its intricate beadwork is still intact. On occasion, I take the now-faded gown out of its dusty cardboard box and marvel at her loving attention to detail. The fine stitches marked the seconds, the minutes, and the hours she spent on my happiness. I cannot bear to discard the wedding dress. I look at it now and I feel fortunate that I have preserved a few precious moments in time.

Aunt Sug, like my grandmother, suffered dementia in her later years. She died in 2002. I could not bear to go to her funeral. I was afraid my insides would burst from grief. So my homage to her is to remain the keeper of all things Seely, just as she would have wished. She left me many gifts, some made of silk organza, many made of paper, and some of molded silver and gold. To this day, I cherish a delicate, silver-plated pocket mirror and comb set she gave me one Christmas. I carry the small vanity set in my handbag when I attend the theatre and in some strange way, Aunt Sug is with me enjoying the show. She would likely smile and say that music can bring us great comfort and joy. I treasure her worn blue and floral silk jewelry pouches and her evening emerald peridot birthstone that still sparkles. But it is her lovely soprano voice that echoes in my ear and her steadfast family pride that swells in my heart that I cherish the most. She felt that each of us decides what our dreams are made of, and we can become a star and write our own press releases.

Aunt Sug on my wedding day in 1985.
She worked on my gown for months.

The Skinny House was transferred out of our family a long time ago. I have a few artifacts: a blueprint, a handful of mementos, fading photographs, and a few drafting instruments that my Grandfather Nathan treasured. Part of my loss is my own fault. I remember with a heavy heart the day in 1986 when Mom, Dad, and I were cleaning out Lillian's house after she died. I had driven down from Boston to help them empty her house and collect items I thought dear and worth keeping.

I still hear my mother's question. "Do you want these?" She pointed to a box taken from the Skinny House library that contained some of my grandfather's dusty, musty Seely Bros., Inc. work ledgers. His ledgers had lived in the house all this time. I shook my head and replied no, thinking the ledgers looked too heavy, dirty, and musty to save. *Why would I want those?* I thought. Besides, I had no more room in my small compact car. Looking back, I feel so ashamed that I dumped a precious portion of Nathan's legacy on the street like garbage. I was given the choice to save a part of my family's legacy and I still said no. It was a hard and sad lesson to learn.

Of course Nathan's brochure *Homes for Colored People* binds him, my grandmother, father, and Aunt Sug to me forever. Perhaps telling their stories can make up in part for the mistakes I made underestimating the value of my family's legacy.

More important than physical items, it is the colorful tapestry of memories and anecdotes handed down that I treasure the most. From these I have learned some important life lessons. People speak of these life lessons as *generational gifts* or *inter-generational gifts*, intangible wisdom handed down from one generation to another. This process of spiritual binding between us and our grandparents and parents despite the years or decades that have separated us can give way to ancestral healing.

Nathan was a driven man who managed to salvage the silver lining of a crisis not of his own making. His innate talent and inner drive to build things salvaged his self-esteem. He may have failed to convince Lillian that their hard times were temporary, and he may have thought that his business could rebound if she had more faith in him and perhaps if Tom had gone into business with him. However, I believe it was not that simple—and it was too late. His wife and son had moved on with their separate lives.

Nathan's final effort to restore his role as a provider and a builder occurred in 1954 when he was living in West Haven, Connecticut. He was still very much focused on using the talents he had. He purchased a plot of land with the intention of creating a new Seely family estate. Even then, as an old man, he was still hoping against hope that he could rebuild his life, and this time around, include his son and grandchildren. When Nathan offered to give Dad a portion of the lot, Dad declined, passing up an opportunity to become a landowner and another chance to mend fences with his father. However, Aunt Sug did not pass up the deal. She accepted Nathan's offer, and years later sold the West Haven lot and reinvested the money in order to build her custom home in Pawling, New York.

On his future family estate, Nathan sectioned off the lot with surveyor pegs and string. He built a one-room shack on the property, complete with siphoned electricity from the nearby telephone pole lines, another sign of his indefatigable ingenuity. My brother Nate, five years old at the time, recalled his grandfather gave him a cream-colored four-key plastic trumpet. My brother became obsessed with the toy, so much so that when asked a few years later which musical instrument he would like to learn how to play, he chose the trumpet. That one experience with our grandfather, combined with Dad's love for jazz, sparked my brother's lifelong interest in playing the trumpet and his fascination with the famous trumpeter Miles Davis. He became good enough to play in the MIT college jazz band. In my eyes, the toy trumpet that my grandfather gave Nate became a generational gift.

I thank Nathan for teaching me that when I meet someone who has the telltale signs of having had a stroke, I should think of them as a wounded warrior who survived some great battle, some epic crisis in life. I should be curious about who they were before the insult to their brain. Had they conducted a symphony before it happened? Were they right handed, left handed, or ambidextrous? How many times had his or her hand, perhaps now contracted or limp, signed a paycheck in order to support a family or written on a chalkboard in front of a classroom of students? How many extra shifts had they worked to be able to move their kids to a better neighborhood? The one thing I am sure of is that, despite their visible handicap, in their minds, they may still be the architect, the breadwinner, the parent or dedicated teacher. They are still who they always were in spite of their lopsided weakness, use of a cane or wheelchair and in spite of their new residence in a nursing home.

Building a skinny but sturdy house in response to enormous loss is a great lesson. And navigating around boulders, whether literally or figuratively in our paths, as Nathan was able to do, is a positive attribute. We must keep moving, living, and celebrating the good times while trying to survive the bad times. The lesson of Nathan's life is that life is full of contradictions. It is ambidextrous in nature and a balance of successes and failures, often with a hidden silver lining tipping the scales.

My grandfather never let go of his drafting pencil. In one of the last pictures taken of him after his stroke, he is dressed in a suit Aunt Sug bought him. He is gripping a pencil in his contracted right hand in an effort to retain some dignity despite his failing body. There is no hint of a drooping smile. Instead, he flashes a familiar haughty grin reminiscent of the energy and vision of his teenage years, and of the textured richness of his experiences in life. The brain injury rendered him physically handicapped, but by all accounts his mind, and more importantly, his dignity were intact.

Maybe there are other lessons from his life and career. While Nathan was a visionary entrepreneur, he was also a vulnerable, fallible man. He believed his son, Tom, should have learned a trade in the building business. That was a rational choice for his generation. The idea of apprenticeship was a core American value in the 1900s. Fathers customarily passed on their trade to their sons. My father had another option—college. Today, we would add the fields of science, technology, engineering, and mathematics (STEM) education[80] to the list of the basic group of trades such as excavating, carpentry, and machinery.

It's been said that a man's ego adheres to his life's work. That being the case, there is a high price to pay when you are unemployed and broke: loss of self-esteem, marital anguish, and the exhaustion of keeping up appearances. If a man's work defines his identity, my grandfather was a builder until the day he died. He was a carpenter long after his ability to strike a nail had faded.

My grandfather Nathan T. Seely Sr. recuperating after a stroke at a rehabilitation facility in New York. ca. 1958-62.

The working title of this book was *Ambidextrous*, and not just because I learned my grandfather could write with either hand. There were parallel stories here about two men who were polar opposites. One man I never met, and the other I saw every day of my life. I have come to terms with my father's discomfort with the spotlight and my grandfather's relishing in it. I got to know a creative, resilient grandfather who thrived in the face of limitations, and a more troubled son who kept secrets, lost self-respect, and despaired for much of his adolescence.

I learned that there could be a story behind a person who is frowned upon by others, as Nathan was by my father. My grandfather was confident and saw his glass as half full. When challenged by financial ruin, he decided to rebuild his life. In contrast, my father, Tom, cautious and introspective, viewed his father as too much of a risk taker. Through no fault of his own, as an adolescent he never appreciated Nathan's perspective as a progressive black entrepreneur in the 1920s. He never appreciated the financial risks and personal sacrifices his father made in order to take care of his family and to keep a roof over their heads. My father's lack of insight into his own father's situation is understandable. Children are only dimly aware of things that go on with parents. They're curiosity seekers. They know just a little growing up and have questions later in life. Their personal perspective often seems light years from that of their parents.

It is likely that my father was not privy to the intimacy and commitment of his parents. Nathan and Lillian married in 1915, but most of what my father had witnessed growing up was their losses: loss of livelihood, loss of home, and loss of pride. The chronic tension in the household must have been palpable. Perhaps my father should not be blamed for failing to embrace Nathan's gift: the blood, sweat, and tears that went into building the Skinny House. Nor can I blame my father or grandfather for not appreciating Lillian's upwardly mobile determination, her grit, and her defiance to settle for anything less. I empathize with her anger at Nathan but also wish she could have forgiven him.

My grandfather Nathan Thomas Seely Sr., at age sixty-nine, died of complications of a stroke in at Hudson River State Hospital in Poughkeepsie on November 2, 1962. He was buried without a grave marker in the White Plains Rural Cemetery. His obituary included the final moving stanza of William Cullen Bryant's famous poem about death, *Thanatopsis*.

> So live, that when thy summons comes to join
> The innumerable caravan that moves
> To that mysterious realm, where each shall take
> His chamber in the silent halls of death,
> Thou go not, like the quarry-slave at night,
> Scourged to his dungeon, but, sustained and soothed,
> By an unfaltering trust, approach thy grave
> Like one who wraps the drapery of his couch
> About him and lies down to pleasant dreams.[81]

We plan to place a headstone to mark his grave that reads: *So I lived and so I built. Now I lie down to pleasant dreams.*

My father "bequeathed" to me a few calculus books, an outdated set of *World Book* encyclopedias, his "wannabe" conductor's baton, a stack of Broadway sheet music, and a tattered copy of *The Rubaiyat of Omar Khayyam*, a gift in 1969 by a grateful Iranian student at Morgan State. And I still have my Winter & Co. upright piano, acquired in the summer of 1956. I treasure these items so much.

My father's life experiences have taught me that decisions I make to survive a crisis can affect the people I love and those I am trying to protect. My father's determined quest to go to college helped me realize that the right choice may mean deferring a dream until all the ducks have been lined up. He faced many obstacles, yet he persevered. His academic achievements instilled in me a love of education, a treasure beyond bankruptcy. Education can never be taken away. Family is important. Other things should rank highly too, such as the personal standards we create, live by, and strive to maintain. We should believe in our educational goals, whether supported by some or none; and believe in our achievements, whether they are inspired by some or lauded by no one.

My father's experience growing up in the Skinny House made me realize that it should never matter how big or how small a house is. What matters is where your heart resides, and whether you have made that house into a home.

In retrospect, if I added up all the time my father had spent with his feet propped up in his worn recliner or parked on the piano bench, it would be years. In fact, I feel that his sedentary lifestyle contributed to his heart failure and needing open-heart surgery in 1978. As his illness progressed, his fatigue worsened even at rest. I had the unfortunate experience of performing CPR on him after he had just been released from the hospital. I talked with him through the small window in the ambulance during the ride to the hospital, and I held his hand while he lay on the gurney in the emergency room. He survived for a few more weeks. I will never forget the sad, resigned look on his face when I asked how he was doing. "I am waiting for my last breath," he said.

I wanted to comfort him, but all I could muster at the time was to smile and say, "Oh, Daddy, you're going to be fine."

In 1989, one month before he died, my father wrote out the lyrics to a love song called "I'm Stone in Love With You," written by Thom Bell, Linda Creed, and Anthony Bell, made popular by the Stylistics and later covered by Johnny Mathis. Below the soulful stanza he wrote to my mother, "This is how I feel about you." It is hard for me to think of my parents, especially my father, as a passionate man and vulnerable lover. As kids, we only saw the box of Whitman chocolates he gave my mother on Mother's Day, the Hallmark card addressed to "My Ol' Lady" on Valentine's Day, or the ugly pair of brown gloves he gave her every Christmas. In hindsight, my mother accepted my father's limitations in expressing his love. It was okay that he borrowed song lyrics and regifted them to her.

Mom and Dad heading out to a Johnny
Mathis concert in Baltimore. 1982

My mother still has the paper with the song lyrics on it. It is one of the rare gifts from her, at times, emotionally unavailable husband. She told us that he kissed her good night every night of their married life. I believe her.

The only anniversary gift I gave to my parents that I consider perfect were front row tickets to a 1988 Johnny Mathis concert at the Meyerhoff Symphony Hall in Baltimore. My mother believed in her heart that Johnny sang directly to her.

In the last few months of his life, my father was weak and confined to his bedroom. We were not surprised when, toward the end, he requested his favorite appetizer, Oysters Rockefeller. We had grown up sharing his love for late-night snacks, such as crackers with blue cheese and pepperoni, or raw clams with hot sauce. Nate and Robbie prepared a feast for him, but he managed to eat only a few forkfuls of food.

During the last days of his life, my father spent a lot of time alone with Nate, who has never to this day divulged what they shared. I know he had forgiven Dad for missing his MIT graduation. In the final hours of his life, Dad asked Mom whether she thought she would have had a better life if she had married someone else. He wanted to know if he had made her happy. She assured him that he had. After a conversation with the woman he had loved for forty-eight years, he seemed to let go, just as if he were lying down to a pleasant dream. Watching my parents at the end, I realized that my mother was my father's Rock of Gibraltar, and not the other way around. No matter how many debates she conceded to him during their years of marriage, she remained his most ardent supporter.

Dad died at the age of sixty-eight of heart failure on February 21, 1989. He had lived to see me graduate from medical school. He had spent time with two of his grandchildren, Thomas and Helen. But he had never met his granddaughter Diane or my son Devereaux. I am sure he would have taught my son how to play the piano and would have been elated that Diane majored in mathematics in college.

We cremated his remains. There was no formal church ceremony or any elaborate service to celebrate his life. We had a simple spaghetti dinner in his honor, and we twirled and slurped his favorite meal. He would have been satisfied by our celebration, but I came away feeling empty and thought that we had not done enough to honor him. My grief was not assuaged. After all, my father was the smartest man I knew and most devoted to his family.

When we finished our spaghetti dinner, an elderly relative, Aunt Inie, who was respected for her quiet words of wisdom, leaned over and whispered to me, " We have to let him go or he will not rest in peace." We let Dad go. In 1992 we combined his ashes with Michael's and sprinkled father and son under an apple tree in Connecticut.

Looking back, I realize my grandfather Nathan Seely and my father Tom Seely were not perfect. In their early years, they lived in sync, moving on parallel tracks. In later life, they moved in opposite directions. They each made mistakes. Sadly, they never resolved their differences or made peace with each other, though they were both resilient and seemed capable of doing so. Their life stories prove that a country's economic crisis affects each family member differently and to succeed against all odds, ingenuity is required.

I initially judged both men incorrectly. I had to rebalance the scales and find a truer sense of each man. For a long time, I idealized my grandfather. Now I see him as less mythic and realize he had large flaws. His pride impeded his ability to survive a marriage shattered by financial ruin. In his mind, carpentry and building were all he was meant to do in life. He left the family when they needed him the most. He loved his family, yet had a tough time expressing it.

My father's shame over the Skinny House obscured important truths in my life. His shame spawned my disapproval. His shame made me feel that he had not lived up to many of his family's expectations. He had not met Nathan's expectation that he seek a career building houses. He had not met Lillian's expectation that he help her return to the grand house. He thwarted Aunt Sug's expectation that he marry a "worldly" woman. He had not met my mother's expectation that he take every promotion offered to him throughout his career. He might even have disappointed himself by not getting his PhD in mathematics. Until recently, I thought of my father as the "weaker" man. This has changed.

I realize my father had a crushing blow at a vulnerable age, and a really hard time when his parents broke up. But he overcame those things. This is impressive. I see him now as a strong, yet vulnerable, man who became depressed when his father left. He rebounded and built a successful life, following what he knew would work and in the face of criticism all around. He survived the Great Depression, got a college education, married the woman he loved, and raised a family. He took his obligations as husband and father seriously. These two responsibilities in his life trumped getting a PhD, trumped living in a bigger house, or accepting every job promotion. My father was fulfilled holding a book in one hand and a baby in the other. He was ambidextrous in that unique way.

If I could direct a movie that captured Nathan and Tom, my grandfather would be the guy pushing to be the first in line to preview it. He would be asking himself, *I wonder if I could have produced this movie?* My father would be the guy checking the movie reviews first before deciding whether to wait in line to see a movie he probably would not like. I feel lucky to be related to both men.

Where would I be in the film? I have inherited a little of both personalities. I have pushed past the innate shyness I inherited from my father. I have accepted that it makes me uncomfortable to be around a lot of unfamiliar people. Despite my preference for dim lights, I always manage to stay in line to see the movie. Like my grandfather, I would be closer to the front of the line. Like him, I have taken risks in my life and career. I have failed in a few business ventures and consider it no big deal to get up off the ground, dust myself off, and try again. I have succeeded in life and career. More importantly, I raised a responsible, loving son who will pass on his great-grandfather and grandfather's legacies.

My grandfather and father have been my spiritual companions for the past several years. They have traveled with me everywhere. Nathan invites himself for dinner and never fails to bring up the subject of the house. He whispers, "Are you really going to tell them about my house?" He was my passenger during the long commutes from the green suburbs of West Chester, Pennsylvania, to the steely horizon of Philly's Center City. He urged me to stop daydreaming, to turn off the radio, and to concentrate on what would be in the next chapter of this book. I have moved to northern Virginia and he still hounds me. As I whiz down Dulles Toll Road, he nudges me to tell this or that anecdote. He reminds me that, unless I write the story down, a little part of him will die again. He takes up a lot of my free time and seems to be very proud of that fact.

My father, on the other hand, is my backseat driver. He ignores the authoritative female voice of the GPS. As an armchair politician and overly cautious parent, he objects to my project. "Wait a minute," he says. "Hold on. Slow down. What direction are you going with this story?" His face is as red as a beet. "One of these days, I will tell you about that house at 175 Grand Street...one of these days," he promises.

In 2009, I took my grandfather's blueprint of the Skinny House to a framer's shop in suburban Philadelphia. I chose this particular shop because its walls were covered with pictures and paintings regal enough to hang in any fine museum. The shop's owner helped me choose a classic burl wood frame for the blueprint. When I returned a few weeks later to pick it up, the shop owner was out and his assistant helped me. She meticulously unwrapped it. For a few moments, we stared at the blueprint in silence. After a minute, she politely informed me that Nathan's drafted measurements were off by a quarter inch. For a split second, I was peeved at her "mountain out of a molehill" observation. I considered the blueprint a rare, precious artifact. In the end, I had to admit that her comment was correct, yet ironically befitting of Nathan's legacy.

We know so little if we just look at the appearance of the blueprint. Yes, the blueprint's measurements are off, and yes, the architect was an imperfect man. However, the shop clerk did not know that, in 1931, Nathan's valiant efforts went into every "imperfect" detail of every nook and cranny of this small, cozy home. She did not know the smudge in the corner of the drawing is sweat, the imprint of an entrepreneur who envisioned building homes for poor blacks escaping racism. The smudge is the residue of a devastated man who built a special house with his last ounce of pride. She did not know the story of my grandmother Lillian, a devoted parent who humbled herself to support her children. She did not know of my father's triumphant journey to get a college education, to marry, and to raise children who loved him. She did not know of my Aunt Sug's resilience, love for opera, and zest for life. She was unaware that this blueprint anchors my family's legacy on a neck of land called *Mamaroneck, a place where the sweet waters fall into the sea.* If she had known all of these things, she would have understood that this blueprint of a skinny house is perfect.

THE END

Epilogue

Brick and Mortar of a Soul

For several years, the blueprint of the Skinny House hung on my dining room wall. When saying grace over dinner, I was reminded of Nathan's favorite saying before eating: "Now, let's have a nice get-together." I keep the *Homes for Colored People* brochure displayed under glass and eagerly show it with pride to visitors. However soon both the blueprint and the brochure may have a new home. The Smithsonian National Museum of African American History and Culture in Washington, D.C.[82] has expressed interest in obtaining my collection of memorabilia related to Nathan's skinny house.

I wish the Skinny House could be easily preserved like a blueprint or a brochure. Unfortunately, that is not the case for brick and mortar. In September 2013, Nancy Picarello, the current owner of the Skinny House, called me. She had rented out the house for many years, and when her tenant moved out, she began renovations. Her contractor discovered severe termite damage to a portion of the kitchen floorboards and east wall. The house, built in an area with a high water table and damp conditions, was primed for termite infestation. The structural damage to the kitchen was extensive. I had to face reality that our cherished house, the symbol of my grandfather's legacy, may not last forever.

I was devastated. I felt as if I were losing my grandfather's house all over again and was helpless to do anything about it. This time I was facing a formidable enemy, Mother Nature. For the first time, the Skinny House was structurally vulnerable and, I feared, mortally wounded.

Devereaux and I examined the holes in the belly of the foundation. We touched splintered beams and lamented the laxity of her steel cables, once taut like lasers. I insisted on climbing her steep staircase to the third-level bedroom just to make sure the village vista remained. I was relieved to find the church steeples still there, just barely capping the treetops. Despite her dusty rooms, missing floorboards, and disrupted sheetrock, I still loved the old place. I could not hold back tears later that night. I cried for my grandfather. Had anyone ever praised him for trying to build a business in 1923? I cried for my father, finally understanding his heartache. I cried as a daughter, knowing that Dad, in spite of his feelings about the house, would be proud of me standing there with his grandson. The question then became, what are we going to do to save this special house?

In January 2015, the New York State Office of Parks, Recreation and Historic Preservation and I worked together to secure the Skinny House a spot on the National Register of Historic Places. At the time, in Mamaroneck, there were only four buildings with this designation: the Mamaroneck United Methodist and St. Thomas Episcopal churches, known for their gothic architecture; Walter's Hot Dog Stand, famous for its pagoda-style roof; and the colonial-styled Albert E. and Emily Wilson House. The Skinny House was deserving of the coveted fifth spot, and that happened on May 18, 2015.[83] As far as I know, my grandfather's house is the only ten-foot-wide, three-story, single-family home built out of salvaged materials by an African-American man in the United States.

The four great-grandchildren of Nathan T. Seely Sr. are millennial adults now. They revere the grandfather and great-grandfather whom they have never met. They all embrace the tiny house movement and a smaller carbon footprint with a do-it-yourself (DIY) ethic. For them a home is a home, and everyone deserves one, even if you have to build it yourself. They feel Nathan was ahead of his time.

My son Devereaux, a website designer, is twenty-something years old now. It took an elementary school assignment for us to discover the true story of his great-grandfather's famous house. He silk-screened a portrait of the house and it hangs right next to the Nathan's blueprint. My niece Diane followed in my father's footsteps and is a mathematician. She works for an IT company that designs software for building construction. I imagine Nathan's jaw would drop to know we now use computers to design blueprints and to navigate construction sites. My other niece, Helen, is an educational advocate for an international non-profit organization dedicated to supplementing classroom lessons with teaching entrepreneurial skills. My nephew Thomas, a radio-journalist, writes about culture and the arts. Oh, how proud my father and grandfather would be.

As for me, my work to help preserve the Skinny House continues. I would like to have the house returned to the Seely family ownership long enough for it to be restored, then transferred to a non-profit entity that will protect and preserve it for the next generation of history-seekers. Partial proceeds from the sale of this book will be used to make charitable donations to STEM and music education programs, historical societies, and colleges dear to the Seely family. My grandfather and father would be pleased to know that their legacies live on at institutions of education, innovation, and historical preservation.

Julie L. Seely
March 2018

Addenda

Homes for
Colored
People

A Personal Message for

THE EAGLE PUBLICATIONS
WHITE PLAINS, N. Y.

The Colored Man's Home

VERY colored man needs a home. That statement does not require proof. It is the dearest wish of every individual of every color or race to have a clean, decent place in which to house his family, in which to bring up his children in peace and comfort.

But there has been a great increase in recent years in the colored population of the North. This has brought with it a very serious housing problem. No longer is it easy for the colored man to find, at the price he can afford to pay, a decent place in which to live.

Nor can he look to the white man for assistance. That individual has his own troubles; he is too busy making a living for his own family to worry about the difficulties of any other race. The colored people must work out their own problem; they must help each other. It is for that great purpose that Seely Brothers, Inc., has been organized. It will supply colored people everywhere with homes.

The Story of a Great Purpose

Two or three years ago there were living in the Village of Mamaroneck two young colored men, Nathan T. Seely and Willard Seely. They had no great amount of worldly goods, but they were hardworking and they had a good reputation. With these they started in business.

To them came the great vision of what they could accomplish for their own race by supplying it with homes. To this end they started the erection of an apartment house. It was not easy at first. They had to work hard; they had many discouragements, but nothing stopped them. No matter what happened they kept on working. They never admitted defeat and in the end success crowned their efforts. The time has been short, but, already they have accomplished wonderful things.

Today they own considerable real property in Mamaroneck. More than that they have built up a big business. They have purchased much labor-saving machinery to use in future operations. Among these things are trucks, tractors, power driven saws, and wood-working machinery, everything, in short, that is needed to do their work cheaply and efficiently. In this little booklet are pictures of some of the things they now own.

More important than all this is the position they have made for themselves in the Village in which they live. By honesty and hard work they have brought themselves to the point where they are considered among the substantial citizens of the community, without regard to race or color. They have the respect of all who know them for they have earned it.

The Purpose of Seeley Bros., Inc.

Now they desire to increase their business; they wish to accomplish more and better things. For this purpose, therefore, they have associated with themselves several other prominent colored men of White Plains and vicinity. Among them are A. R. Davis, Rev. W.. H Edwin Smith, Pastor of the Second Baptist Church, and J. A. Blythe.

These men have organized a corporation known as Seely Brothers, Inc. It will have a capital stock of $100,000. This will be divided into 5,000 shares of preferred stock paying a dividend of 8%, having a par value of $10 per share, and 10,000 shares of common stock having a par value of $5 per share.

It is the purpose of the company to supply homes for colored people. Apartment houses, stores, lodge rooms, amusement halls, one and two family houses will be erected or bought. Tracts of land will be bought and divided into building lots. These properties will be rented and sold, bringing in revenue to the company.

The building and machinery now owned by the Seely Brothers will be turned over to the corporation. This will give the new company the tools with which to work and will bring in money from the start. The company will receive rents from the buildings already owned by it of $3,600 a year.

Part of the preferred stock of the company is now being offered for sale to a selected list of colored people. It sells for $10 per share and pays interest at the rate of 8% per year, twice that paid by a savings bank. In addition to this, with each share of preferred stock will be given free a share of common stock of the par value of $5 per share. Among the holders of this common stock will be divided all the additional earnings of the company. These should be very large.

Don't you want to join with the men whose names have been given in this booklet and aid in the great work? Remember, if you do you will be sure of two things :—

First: You will greatly aid your own colored race by supplying it with homes.

Second: You will make money for yourself.

Right now while you are thinking about it mail the enclosed postal card to us. That will cost you nothing and may give you a chance to make a lot of money. You will be under no obligation to us whatever by mailing the card. But we will send our representative to see you and tell you all about Seely Brothers, Inc., and the chance it offers you to help the colored people and at the same time make money.

APARTMENT HOUSE OWNED BY
SEELY BROTHERS, INC.

TWO FAMILY HOUSE, NOW BUILDING,
OWNED BY SEELY BROTHERS, INC.

SEELY BROS., Inc.
95 S. Lexington Ave.
White Plains, N. Y.

Bibliography

Books

Brackbill, Eleanor Phillips. *An Uncommon Cape: Researching the Histories and Mysteries of a Property*. New York: SUNY Press, 2012.

Galbraith, John Kenneth. *The Great Crash 1929*. New York: Houghton Mifflin Harcourt, 2009.

Gray, Brenda Clegg. *Black Female Domestics During the Depression in New York City, 1930–1940*. New York: Garland, 1993.

Green, Nelson. Article: Oscar LeRoy Warren in *History of the Valley of the Hudson: River of Destiny*, 1609-1930. Vol: 5, 1931, pp. 341-343, retrieved from New York State Library on 7/12/2015 by Jennifer Betsworth, New York State Office of Parks and Recreation and Historic Preservation.

Greenberg, Cheryl Lynn. *To Ask for an Equal Chance: African-Americans in the Great Depression*. Lanham, MD: Rowman & Littlefield, 2009.

Hughes, Lyn. *An Anthology of Respect: The Pullman Porter's National Registry of African American Railroad Employees*, Chicago, IL: Hughes Peterson Publishing, 2007.

Keller, Lisa. "Dreams Delivered: Following Diversity's Path in Westchester." In *Westchester: The American Suburb*. Edited by Roger Panetta. New York: Fordham University Press, 2006. pp. 327–343.

Motley, Constance Baker. *Equal Justice Under Law: An Autobiography.* New York: Farrar, Straus and Giroux, 1998.

Murolo, Priscilla. "Domesticity and Its Discontents." In *Westchester: The American Suburb.* Edited by Roger Panetta. New York: Fordham University Press, 2006. pp. 345–373.

Daniel Okrent. *Last Call: The Rise and Fall of Prohibition.* New York: Scribner, 2010.

Panetta, Roger. "Westchester, the American Suburb: A New Narrative." In *Westchester: The American Suburb.* Edited by Roger Panetta New York: Fordham University Press, 2006. pp. 5–75.

Taylor, Nick. *American-Made, The Enduring Legacy of the WPA: When FDR Put the Nation to Work.* New York: Bantam Dell, A Division of Random House, Inc., 2008.

Troetel, Barbara. "Suburban Transportation Defined: America's First Parkway." In *Westchester: The American Suburb.* Edited by Roger Panetta. New York: Fordham University Press, 2006. pp. 247–289.

Wiese, Andrew. *Places of Their Own: African American Suburbanization in the Twentieth Century.* Chicago: The University of Chicago Press, 2005.

Wilkerson, Isabel. *The Warmth of Other Suns: The Epic Story of America's Great Migration.* New York: Vintage, 2010.

Williams, Gray. "Westchester County: Historic Suburban Neighborhoods." In *Westchester: The American Suburb*. Edited by Roger Panetta. New York: Fordham University Press, 2006. pp. 179–215.

Property Assessment Records: Village of Mamaroneck, N.Y.

Liber 4438, p. 279, recorded 9/17/1946.

Liber 4468, p. 83, recorded 11/29/1946.

Liber 4537, p. 193, recorded 7/14/1947.

Liber 4871, p. 130, recorded 6/23/1950.

Westchester County Land Records: Town of Mamaroneck

Liber 2251, Apr 23, 1920, p. 246.

Liber 2417, Apr 5, 1923, p. 351.

Liber 2469, Dec 6, 1923, p. 293.

Liber 2525, Jun 23, p. 218.

Liber 2558, Sept 9, 1926, p. 46.

Liber 2583, Jun 23, 1925, p. 151.

Liber 2622, Feb 2, 1927, p. 216.

Liber 2718, Nov 9, 1926, p. 315.
Liber 2718, Nov 9, 1926, p. 316.

Liber 2764, May 10, 1927, p. 179.

Liber 2773, Jun 13, 1927, pp. 282–283.

Liber 2961, Mar 17, 1929, p. 249.

Liber 2962, Aug 8, 1929, p. 476.

Liber 2962, Oct 6, 1927, p. 402.

Liber 2965, Sept 1929, p. 238.

Liber 2968, Aug 8, 1929, p. 238

Liber 3036, May 17, 1930, p. 399.

Liber 3086, Oct 8, 1930, p. 244.

Liber 3190, Oct 28, 1930, p. 464.

Liber 3833, May 28, 1940, p. 105.

Liber 3864, Sept 25, 1940, p. 351.

Liber 4468, Nov 29, 1946, p. 83.

Liber 4537, Jul 14, 1947, pp. 193, 195, 197.

Liber 4541, Jul 25, 1947, p. 196.
Liber 4871, Jun 23, 1950, p. 130.

Westchester County Archives, New Rochelle, NY, A-0303 (417) L folder, File No. 1906-762. 8/19/1907. Surrogate's Court, County of Westchester. In the Matter of the Judicial Settlement of the Account of Proceedings of New Rochelle Trust Company as Administrator of Charles G. Seely, Deceased.

Westchester Court Records: The Richardson Realty & Construction Co., Inc. Certificate of Incorporation, A0050 (42), Sept 12, 1922, pp. 34–36.

Westchester County Court Records, Certificate of Incorporation of Seely Brothers, Inc., April 18, 1925. A-0050 (50), p. 470.

Westchester County Archives: Jail Blotter Records for Oscar LeRoy Warren. Index: AO412 (20): 1526.

Westchester County Inventory of Historic Places Certificate for the Skinny House, March 1991.

Newspaper and Magazine Articles

Crean, Ellen. "Scenes from Our Gang." *Daily Times* (Mamaroneck Gannett Westchester Newspapers), January 20, 1980.

The Crisis 31, no. 5 (1926).

Dinuzzo, Emily. *Westchester's "Skinny House" Considered for Landmark Status* at westchestermagazine.com retrieved Aug 8, 2015.

Ducati, Marilyn. Poem-Half House in article "Mamaroneck's Beauty in Picture and Verse, Half House." *Daily Times* (Mamaroneck edition Gannett Westchester Newspapers) Mon, Sept 10, 1973.

Gorman, Gail. "Skinny House Gets Landmark Designation." *Daily Times* (Mamaroneck edition Gannett Westchester Newspapers) Tues, Jan 28, 1986.

Grassi, Joseph R. Jr. "Narrow House Receives Wide Attention." *New York Times*, (NY), Sun, Aug 11, 1985.

James, Sandra. "Once Upon a Time, There Was a Skinny House." *Daily Times* (Mamaroneck, Gannett Westchester Newspapers) Apr 1985.

Leven, Diane. "Housing Squeeze Doesn't Bother Her." *Daily Times* (Mamaroneck edition Gannett Westchester Newspapers) Oct 15, 1982.

"Nathan T. Seely Jr., Skinny House Builder Dies at 68." *Daily Times* (Mamaroneck edition Gannett Westchester Newspapers) Mar 30, 1989.

"Real Estate and Building." *Mamaroneck Paragraph,* 1923. Microfilm, Mamaroneck Public Library.

"Reflections of Black History." *Sun-Reporter.*

Pero, James. Skinny House Listed to Historic Registry in *Mamaroneck Review* (Mamaroneck, NY) June 12, 2015, p. 6.

Reisman, Phil. "Mamaroneck's Skinny House, A Symbol of Cooperation in Nation's Darkest Hour" (webcast video). Sept 12, 2013. Lohud.com.

Reisman, Phil. "Skinny House, Fat with History." *Journal News* (Mamaroneck, Gannett Westchester Newspapers), June 2002.

Reisman, Phil. "Tourists Add to Thin House Myths." *Daily Times* (Gannett Westchester Newspapers), Mon, Dec 4, 1978.

"Real Estate and Building." *Mamaroneck Paragraph,* 1923. Microfilm, Mamaroneck Public Library.

"Reflections of Black History." *Sun-Reporter.*

Photo, Courtesy of Joe Bergansky, Portfolio 1978, Howard Publications of Mamaroneck.

Article by Mitch Broder, Gannett Newspaper, June 15, 1994.

Newspaper Articles Regarding Oscar LeRoy Warren

"Oscar Warren, Prominent Lawyer, Missing." *Herald Statesman* (Yonkers, NY) Jan 26, 1933. P1, 13, retrieved Feb 29, 2015 from www.Fultonhistory.com

"Estate Data Now In Hands of Official." *Daily Argus* (Mt. Vernon, NY) Thurs, Feb 2, 1933, p1, retrieved Feb 29, 2015 from www.fultonhistory.com

"Widow Alleges Warren Fraud By Mortgage." *Herald Statesman* (Yonkers, NY) Wed May 10, 1933, p7, retrieved Feb 29, 2015 from www.fultonhistory.com

"Bonding Firm To Make Good Estate Deficit." *Herald Statesman* (Yonkers, NY) Tues, April 11, 1933, p10, retrieved Feb 29, 2015

"Can't Sell Books to Pay Creditors." *Brooklyn Daily Eagle* (Brooklyn, NY). Fri, May 11, 1934. P2, retrieved Feb 7, 2016 from newspapers.com

In The Matter of Oscar Leroy Warren, Attorney, Appellate Division of the Supreme Court of New York, Second Department, 242 App. Div. 649 (N.Y. App Div. June 1934), retrieved from www.casetext.com on Nov 29, 2015.

"Parole Release Probable for Oscar Warren." *Herald Statesman*, (Yonkers, NY) Fri, May 10, 1935, retrieved from www.fultonhistory.com on Feb 29, 2015

"Public Defender at Sing Sing Released." *Dunkirk Evening Observer* (Dunkirk, New York). Wed, Jun 5, 1935. P11, retrieved Nov 29, 2015 from newspapers.com

SEELY FAMILY ARCHIVES AND RELATED DOCUMENTS

"Nathan Thomas Seely." *Original Data: United States, Selective Service System. World War I Selective Service System Draft Registration Cards, 1917-1918. Washington, D.C.: National Archives and Records Administration.* Source Citation: Westchester County, NY Family History Library Roll Number: 1819189, Draft Board: 4. Source Information: Ancestry.com World War I Draft Registration Card-179, 1917-1918 [database online]. Provo, UT, USA: Ancestry.com Operations Inc., 2005, retrieved 3/17/2012

Nathan Thomas Seely. Original Data: United States Selective Service System. World War II Selective Service System Draft Registration Card-1317, 1942. *(Fourth Registration) for the State of Connecticut.* State Headquarters: Connecticut. Microfilm Series: M1962. Source Information: Ancestry.com World War II Draft Registration Card-1317 [database online]. Provo, UT, USA: Ancestry.com Operations Inc., 2010, retrieved 3/17/2012

Seely Bros., Inc., *Homes for Colored People* (company brochure). Ca. 1925. Private collection of Julie Seely.

Seely, Doris M. Interviews by Julie Seely, 2010–2015.

Seely Family Letters, private collection of Julie Seely.

Seely, Julie, Jennifer Betsworth. "Skinny House, Statement of Significance Summary" in *National Register of Historic Places Application*. February 2015.

Seely, Nathan T. "Blueprint of Skinny House, Nathan Seely Acting as Architect." February 7, 1931. Private collection of Julie Seely.

Seely, Nathan T. "Specifications for A Residence to Be Erected at Mamaroneck, N.Y. for Mrs. Lillian B. Seely, Nathan T. Seely Sr., Acting as Architect." 1926. Private collection of Julie Seely.

United States Federal Census, New York 1880, 1900, 1910, 1920, 1930, 1940.

Julie L. Seely

Video/Documentary

Mamaroneck Historical Society. *The Skinny House, Mamaroneck Historical Landmark*. LMC-TV.org. 1986.

Websites

www.blackpast.org

www.encylcopediaofarkansas.net

www.historyorb.com

www.Legacyproject.org

www.mathforum.org

www.thepeoplehistory.com

www.townofmamaroneck.org

www.village.mamaroneck.ny.us

www.villageoflarchmont.org

www.westchesterclerk.com

Endnotes

Introduction

1   Cheryl L. Greenberg, *To Ask For an Equal Chance: African-Americans in the Great Depression* (Lanham, MD: Rowman & Littlefield, 2009) 1, 21.

Chapter 2

2   Nathan Thomas Seely Original Data: United States Selective Service System. World War II Selective Service System, Draft Registration Card-1317, 1942. (*Fourth Registration for the State of Connecticut.*) State Headquarters: Connecticut. Microfilm Series: M1962. Source Information: Ancestry.com World War II Draft Registration Card-1317 [database online]. Provo, UT, USA: Ancestry.com Operations Inc., 2010, retrieved 3/17/2012.

3   Definition of ambidextrous, Merriam-Webster's Dictionary and Thesaurus, Springfield, Mass, Merriam-Webster, Inc., 2007 paperback edition, p. 25.

4   Definition of mulatto, Merriam-Webster's Dictionary and Thesaurus, Springfield, Mass, Merriam-Webster, Inc., 2007 paperback edition, p. 531

5   Westchester County Archives, New Rochelle, NY, A-0303 (417) L, folder, File No. 1906-762.

6   Thomas C. Fleming, "Phil Randolph and the Pullman Porter," in Article in *Reflections on Black History Series, Sun-Reporter* Newspaper (San Francisco, CA), July 22, 1998.

7   Lyn Hughes, *An Anthology of Respect: The Pullman Porter's National Registry of African American Railroad Employees* (Chicago, IL: Hughes Peterson Publishing, 2007).

Chapter 3

8   Edward Floyd De Lancey, Esq., "Mamaroneck," in *History of Westchester County*, vol. 1, ed. John Thomas Scharf (New York: L. E. Preston & Company, 1886), 846.

9   Ibid. 849.

10   Ibid. 849.

11   Roger Panetta, Editor, "Westchester: The American Suburb" in *Westchester: The American Suburb* (New York: Fordham University Press, 2006), 51.

12   George A. Lundberg, Mirra Komarovsky, and Mary Alice McInery, "Appendices: Table X–Population Characteristics of Four Types of Suburban Population," in *Leisure: A Suburban Study* (New York: Columbia University Press, 1934).

13   Andrew Wiese, *Places of Their Own: African American Suburbanization in the Twentieth Century* (Chicago: University of Chicago Press, 2004), 23–25.

14   Ellen Crean, "Scenes from Our Gang in Article: Sound View," Mamaroneck (NY) *Daily Times*, Jan 20, 1980.

Chapter 4

15   "Rate of Wages Per Hour Being Paid in the Building Trades," *American Contractor* 41 (April 3, 1920): 31.

16   CPI Inflation Calculator, Bureau of Labor Statistics, www.data.bls.gov.

17   The Richardson Realty & Construction Co., Inc. Certificate of Incorporation, Westchester Court Records: A0050 (42), Sept 12, 1922, pp. 34–36.

18   Westchester County Land Records: Town of Mamaroneck, Liber 2251, April 23, 1920, p. 246.

19   Mamaroneck Paragraph: Real Estate & Building, 1923, Microfilm at Mamaroneck Public Library.

20   Westchester County Land Records, Town of Mamaroneck, Liber 2469, Dec 6, 1923, p. 293.

21   Willford Isbell King, "Table 7, Estimated Numbers of Employees, 1920–1927." *The National Income and Its Purchasing Power* (New York: National Bureau of Economic Research, 1930), 58–81, www.ssa.gov/history.

22   Westchester County Court Records, Seely Bros., Inc., File A-0050 (50), p. 470.

23   "Estimates of Unemployment in the United States. Variations by Industries" www.ssa.gov/history.

24   Daniel Okrent, *Last Call: The Rise and Fall of Prohibition* (New York, NY: Scribner, 2010).

25   The Deep south is composed of the seven states that formed the original Confederate States of America: Georgia, Florida, Alabama, Mississippi, Louisiana, south Carolina, and Texas.

26   Richard Wormser. The Rise and Fall of Jim Crow: The Harlem Renaissance (1917–1935). Article: *Jim Crow Stories.* www.pbs.org retrieved Jul 5, 2016.

27   W. E. B. DuBois, *The Crisis: A Record of the Darker Races,* (NY) 12, no.6 (1916): 270, digitized at the Modernist Journals Project, www.modjourn.org.

28   W. E. B. DuBois, *The Crisis: A Record of the Darker Races,* (NY) 19, no. 3 (1920), digitized at the Modernist Journals Project, www.modjourn.org.

29   W. E. B. DuBois, "The Year 1925: Segregation," *The Crisis: A Record of the Darker Races* 31 (NY) 1925, No. 5: 229, digitized by Google Books.

30   Jeannie Mitchell, Interview 2012

31   Isabel Wilkerson, *The Warmth of Other Suns: The Epic Story of America's Great Migration* (NY) Random House, 2010.

32   Nathan T. Seely Sr., *Specifications for a Residence to Be Erected at Mamaroneck, New York for Mrs. Lillian B. Seely,* July 5, 1926.

Chapter 6

33   Dan Bryan, *The Great (Farm) Depression of the 1920's,* americanhistoryusa.com, retrieved Oct 4, 2015.

34   Irving Fisher. "The Debt-Deflation Theory of Great Depressions," *Econometrica* 1, no. 4 (1933): 337–57, www.fraser.stlouisfed.org.

35   "Great Depression: Mainstream Explanations: Debt Deflation," Wikipedia.org.

36   Nick Taylor, *American Made: The History of the Works Progress Administration* (NY) Bantam Dell, 2008).

37   Westchester County Land Records, Liber 2764, p. 179.

38   Westchester County Land Records, Liber 2773, pp. 282, 283.

39   Westchester County Land Records, Liber 2962, p. 249.

40   Westchester County Land Records, Liber 2962, p. 476.

41   Westchester County Land Records, Liber 2718, p. 316.

42   Westchester County Land Records, Liber 2622, p. 216.

43   Westchester County Land Records, Liber 3036, p. 399.

44   Westchester County Land Records, Liber 3833, p. 105.

45   Cheryl L. Greenberg, *To Ask for an Equal Chance: African-Americans in the Great Depression* (Lanham, MD: Rowman & Littlefield, 2009). 1, 21

Chapter 7

46   John F. Kennedy, Remarks at the United Negro College Fund, April 12, 1959, Pre-Presidential Papers, Box 92, John F. Kennedy Library.

Chapter 8

47   Creo-Dipt Co. Inc. North Tonawanda, N.Y., Stained Shingles advertisement, 1929

48   Joseph R. Grassi Jr., "Narrow House Receives Wide Attention," *New York Times*, Aug 11, 1985.

Chapter 9

49   Letter from Mme. Mildah Polia-Pathé to Lillian Seely, 1986. Seely Family Archives.

50   Love thy neighbor article in *The Putnam County Times & Republican* newspaper (NY) Thurs. June 18, 1964.

Chapter 10

51   "Missing Attorney Had Transferred Personal Property," *Daily Argus*, Mt. Vernon (NY) January 27, 1933.

52   "Warren Denies Intention To Violate Law" *Herald Statesman,* Yonkers (NY) Fri., May 11, 1934. P29

53   Ibid

54   Cheryl L. Greenberg. *To Ask for an Equal Chance: African-Americans in the Great Depression* (Lanham, MD: Rowman & Littlefield, 2009) 27, 31, 30

55   *Boston Globe* 2011 report summarized a CDC publication in the American Journal of Public Health regarding suicide rates during the Great Depression, 1929-1933.

56   "Educating Apprentices in the Building Trades," *American Contractor* 43, no.1 (January 7, 1922): 23.

Chapter 11

57   "About Lincoln University: A Legacy of Producing," Leaders www.lincoln.edu.

58   "History, Description and Needs," *Catalogue of Lincoln University* (Chester, PA: 40 No. 1 (Jan 1936).

59   Delta Rho Forensic Society, *Lion Yearbook,* (Chester, PA: 1941)

60   Larry S. Gibson, *Young Thurgood: The Making of a Supreme Court Justice* (Amherst, NY: Prometheus, 2012).

61   Ja A. Jahannes, PhD, *WordSong Poets: A Memoir Anthology,* 2011, (Savannah, GA: Turner Mayfield Publishing Company, 1618

Foxhall Rd. Savannah, GA. 31406. ISBN-100984030700.) See commentary on the significance of Lincoln University's "rabble" culture. See also Dr. Jahannes comments editing the book: *An Unfailing Legacy: Chapters in the History of Lincoln University* (Lincoln University, PA: 2012), extracted on 10/23/2016 from www.inmotionmagazine.com.

62   Tom Brokaw, *The Greatest Generation* (New York: Random House, 1998).

63   Philip A. Harriman, "To the Class of 1943," in *Elm Tree: The Classbook of New Haven High School* (New Haven, CT, 1943), 20.

64   Cherisse Jones-Branch, *Segregation and Desegregation.* The Encyclopedia of Arkansas History & Culture. Arkansas State University, www.EncyclopediaofArkansas.net. Retrieved 6/14/2015

65   Ibid. Retrieved 6/14/2015

Chapter 12

66   "University of Arkansas at Pine Bluff: Historical Overview," www.uapb.edu. Retrieved 6/18/2015

67   Lonnie Williams, *Remembrances in Black: Personal Perspectives of the African American Experience at the University of Arkansas, 1940's–2000* (Tuscaloosa, AL: University of Alabama Press, 2012).

68   "University of Arkansas at Pine Bluff: Historical Overview," www.uapb.edu. Retrieved 6/18/2015

69   Diane Dentice, Stephen F. Austin State University. *Ku Klux Klan (After 1900)*. The Encyclopedia of Arkansas History & Culture. www.encyclopediaofarkansas.net. Retrieved 6/20/2015

70   Constance Baker Motley, *Equal Justice Under Law: An Autobiography* (New York: Farrar, Straus and Giroux, 1998), 60.

71   Ibid. p. 130

Chapter 13

72   Anonymous Poem: "Kitchen Prayer of My House" unknown date.

Chapter 14

73   Marilyn Ducati, "Half-House," Mamaroneck's Beauty in Picture and Verse in Mamaroneck (NY) *Daily Times,* Monday, Sept 10, 1973.

74   Phil Reisman, "Tourists Add to Thin House Myths," in the Mamaroneck (NY) *Daily Times*, Sunday, Dec. 4, 1978.

75   Lillian Hidalgo Seely, Letter to the Editor in the Mamaroneck (NY) *Daily Times*, Dec 13, 1978.

76   Gail Gorman, "Skinny House Gets Landmark Designation," Mamaroneck (NY) *Gannett Westchester Newspapers*, Tuesday, Jan 28, 1986.

77   Phil Reisman, "Skinny House Fat with History," *New York Journal News*, June 2002.

Chapter 15

78   Lillian Hidalgo Seely, letter to Julie Seely, Seely Family Archives, Oct 11, 1983.

Chapter 16

79   Definition of legacy, Merriam-Webster's Dictionary and Thesaurus, Springfield, Mass, Merriam-Webster, Inc., 2007 paperback edition.

80   STEM: Science, technology, engineering, and math.

81   William Cullen Bryant, American Poet. Last stanza "Thanatopsis," written circa 1811–1816, originally published by North American Review, Sept 1817. Retrieved from www.poetryfoundation.org

Epilogue

82   The Smithsonian National Museum of African American History and Culture in Washington, DC, opened to the public in September 2016.

83   The National Register of Historic Places, May 18, 2015.

Acknowledgments

MY SISTER AND MOTHER, DIANE and Doris Meloria, remain my inspirations even after their deaths in December 2015 and January 2016, respectively. Diane's spirit guides me with common sense and love. My mother married a headstrong man yet she was a strong person in her own right. I relied on her to fill in the blanks about my grandfather and father, and their relationship. She clarified details of this story and provided perspective, context, and background. She shared intimate feelings about raising our family. Over the years, I have asked her to recount many sad events in her life. She never held back and always delivered uncompromising honesty and compassion for every chapter.

My brothers Nate and Robbie inspire me always. I am so proud of them.

I owe much gratitude to my paternal aunt, Lillian Seely, affectionately known as Aunt Sug, who saved countless family's photographs, labeled them with names and dates, and then organized them in scrapbooks. She chronicled the important milestones in our lives such as marriages, graduations, and career promotions, as well as the mundane events that helped shape us into adults. Thank goodness she had the foresight to preserve the original Seely Bros., Inc. brochure titled *Homes for Colored People,* a key artifact for this story that provided invaluable insight into my grandfather's drive and entrepreneurship. I am grateful to Aunt Sug's daughter-in-law, Mrs. Sylvia Biggs, who sent me additional boxes of Seely memorabilia after Aunt Sug died.

Thanks to the Seely extended family members, especially the cousins I have recently met, including Aunt Yvonne, Andre, Judy, Kenyatta, and those I will meet. I am glad we found each other after all these years. Your faith and prayers for this book have meant a lot to me.

My mother's family—the Sargeants and Huggins of New Haven, Connecticut—inspired my interest in genealogy. I attended many Huggins Clan reunions when I was too young to really appreciate them. I am grateful to my late aunt Enid, a mentor to all of her nieces and nephews. Uncle Ivan, also deceased, was an architect. He helped me understand the details of the blueprint of the Skinny House and gave me some firsthand memories of my grandfather and father. I wished he had lived long enough to see this project come to fruition.

Jeanne Mitchell Ward, my grandfather's niece, shared her experience of growing up in Mamaroneck during the 1930s. I learned a great deal about African-American domestic workers in Mamaroneck and the housing shortage that affected them.

The Santangelos were kind neighbors to my family for more than ninety years. The friendship, particularly between the patriarchs—Panfilo Santangelo, an Italian-American immigrant, and Nathan Seely Sr., a black carpenter—endured during a difficult time in history. The men had mutual respect for each other, and the bond between their families remains strong to this day. I am forever grateful to Ida Santangelo and her daughter, Nancy Picarello, for their kindness, and for loving the Skinny House as much as I do.

Several Mamaroneck residents stand out for recognizing my grandfather's ingenuity and his contribution to the Village of Mamaroneck and the legacy of African-Americans in Westchester County.

In 1990, four years after my grandmother's death, the Skinny House was designated a local historical landmark. This would not have occurred had it not been for Mamaroneck's longtime historian Grace Huntley Pugh, who campaigned tirelessly for the status and made the application to the Mamaroneck Village Board of Trustees. I am forever grateful for her perseverance and recognition of my grandfather's legacy.

Gloria Pritts, Mamaroneck town historian, is an archivist who deserves special mention. For more than a decade, Pritts organized the archives of the Village of Mamaroneck. I am grateful for her contribution to the Mamaroneck Historical Society's documentary on the Skinny House, produced in 1986 by LMC-TV.org.

Donald March, past president of the Mamaroneck Historical Society and Bill Kratinger and Jennifer Betsworth of the New York Parks and Recreation Historic Preservation Office have worked tirelessly to maintain the spotlight on the Skinny House and to preserve other historic structures in Mamaroneck. They were major supporters for nominating the Skinny House for inclusion on the National Register of Historic Places. I am grateful for their support.

Walter Sedovic, principal and CEO of Walter Sedovic Architects, helped me appreciate how my grandfather ensured the historically significant "good bones" of the Skinny House could withstand the test of time—that is, with the advice from an expert preservationist.

For more than twenty years, veteran reporter Phil Reisman of *Gannett News* has written feature articles on the Skinny House, fueling the public's perpetual interest in this story. Thank you.

I would like to thank a few of the legacy-holders of Lincoln University including President Dr. Brenda A. Allen, past Associate Professor Neal Carlson, Alumni Trustee Mrs. Sharman F. Laurence-Wilson and Emeritus Trustee Dr. William E. Bennett. I am so honored to have your support and hope the book serves to highlight Lincoln's incredible legacy.

I would like to thank many folks I have not met but have come to know through the Facebook page titled "I Remember the Skinny House." The Facebook community has attracted hundreds of friends, many who grew up on Grand Street in Mamaroneck and who remember my grandmother as the lady who lived in the "Skinny House."

I have worked with several talented author-editors over the span of this project. They include memoirist Sara Taber, historical fiction writer Claire

Mulligan, author Carolyn Walker, poet-playwright Alison Luterman, and editor Linda Cashdan at The Word Process. All of them supported my raw, jumbled manuscript drafts because they saw some potential in me as a writer. I am grateful for their encouragement and constructive feedback. Marci Clark and Rebbecca Anderle, my managers at Bookfuel.com, were the best conductors an author could have because they propelled this project forward like a freight train.

The professional advice garnered from consultants Joy Butler, Esq., Jennifer Betsworth, New York State researcher-historian, and Gary Rawlins, journalist was invaluable and helped ensure the story's authenticity. Graphic artist Dashton Parham did a wonderful job with the Skinny House logo and illustrations. Joan and Ken from R&R Photography in Rockville, Maryland did an excellent job restoring my old faded photos for this book.

The poems about Mamaroneck by my dear friend Marilyn Ducati have bolstered my love for the Village and my appreciation for its "beauty and prose."

The support of my Wellesley sisters, Rekha and Joanie, both of the class of 1978, have pushed me to finish this project because they know a Wellesley woman can do anything she sets her mind to do.

I owe a special thank you to personal coaches Meadow Lark Washington MSWLC and Dr. Karen Kingsley. These professionals taught me to live my life and that it is none of my business what other people think of me. This advice has served me well over the years.

I have been sustained with prayers from Rev. Iona A. Smith-Nze of Bridgeport, Connecticut and Pastor Tony Ray Smith and the congregation of The Word Church of Ashburn, Virginia.

I am grateful to a talented young actor/writer, wise beyond his years, named Cameron Munson. His inspirational comments on my one-page essay in 2010 encouraged me to write the 2011 screenplay *Skinny House*. We will work together again.

Lastly, I am grateful to the next generation of guardians of the legacy of Nathan Seely—his descendants, whom I love: my son Devereaux Nathan Sterrette, nephew Thomas Graham Seely, and nieces Helen Graham and Diane Meloria Seely. Onward! Make your ancestors proud.

Permissions and Acknowledgments

A Special Thanks to:

Crisis Publishing Co., Inc., the publisher of the National Association for the Advancement of Colored People. January 1920 Crisis Magazine cover and the I RESOLVE CREDO reprinted by permission.

Marilyn Ducati: Half-House, 1973. Poem published in Mamaroneck's Beauty in Picture and Verse in Mamaroneck (NY) Daily Times, Monday, Sept 10, 1973. Poem reprinted by permission of Marilyn Ducati, Pompano Beach, FL

Carla Fallberg: Skinny House, 1975. Sketch published in Mamaroneck, (NY) Daily Times, Dec 4, 1978. Sketch reprinted by permission of Carla Fallberg, Fremont, California

Ja A. Jahannes PhD: Description of rabble culture of Lincoln University, First published in WordSong Poets, A Memoir Anthology, 2011, Turner Mayfield Publishing Company, 1618 Foxhall Rd. Savannah, GA. 31406. ISBN-100984030700. Reprinted by permission of Clara Aguero Ortiz, CEO, J. Rep Jahannes Productions
Lincoln University:

Photograph: Nathan T. Seely Jr., The Lion Yearbook 1949. Reprinted by permission of Lincoln University, (PA).

Description: Delta Rho Forensic Society Debate Team: Excerpts from Lincoln University Bulletin 1936, The Lion Yearbook 1937, Lincoln University (PA).

Suggested Reading

If you would like more information about the historical events covered in this book, or would like to research the origins of your own house, these books can help:

Eleanor Phillips Brackbill. *An Uncommon Cape: Researching the Histories and Mysteries of a Property*. New York: State University of New York, 2012.

Cheryl Lynn Greenberg. *To Ask for an Equal Chance: African-Americans in the Great Depression*. Lanham, MD: Rowman & Littlefield, 2009.

Constance Baker Motley. *Equal Justice Under Law: An Autobiography*. New York: Farrar, Straus and Giroux, 1998.

Daniel Okrent. *Last Call: The Rise and Fall of Prohibition*. New York: Scribner, 2010.

Roger Panetta, editor. *Westchester: The American Suburb*. New York: Fordham University Press, 2006.

Nick Taylor. *American Made: The Enduring Legacy of the WPA*. New York: Bantam Dell, 2008.

Andrew Wiese. *Places of Their Own: African American Suburbanization in the Twentieth Century*. Chicago: The University of Chicago Press, 2005.

Isabel Wilkerson. *The Warmth of Other Suns: The Epic Story of America's Great Migration*. New York: Vintage, 2010.

Index

About the Author

JULIE SEELY IS A GRADUATE of Wellesley College and the Tufts University School of Medicine. Formerly trained as an obstetrician/gynecologist, she now consults in the field of medical administration. Her early writing career focused on developing educational health materials for women. In 2010, she began a second career writing about the legacy of her grandfather, Nathan T. Seely Sr. Her fictional screenplay, *Skinny House*, based on true events, was shortlisted at the 2011 Gotham New York Screen and Film Festival. Upcoming creative projects in production at Skinny House LLC include a picture book for children and a musical inspired by her grandfather's story.

She resides in northern Virginia with her family.

For more information and to arrange for speaking engagements, please visit the website skinnyhouse.org and send an email to Julie@skinnyhouse.org.

Author's Photo Credit: *Cyndy Porter, Style & Photography*

CPSIA information can be obtained
at www.ICGtesting.com
Printed in the USA
LVHW042354030419
612917LV00001B/58